Waterloo 1815

The birth of modern Europe

Campaign • 15

Waterloo 1815

The birth of modern Europe

Geoffrey Wootten

Series editor Lee Johnson • *Consultant editor* David G Chandler

First published in Great Britain in
1992 by Osprey Publishing,
Midland House, West Way, Botley,
Oxford OX2 0PH, UK
44-02 23rd St, Suite 219,
Long Island City, NY 11101, USA
Email: info@ospreypublishing.com

British Library Cataloguing in
Publication Data
Wootten, Geoffrey
Waterloo, 1815: Birth of Modern
Europe. -(Osprey Campaign Series;
v. 15)
I. Title II. Series
940.27
ISBN: 978 1 85532 210 3

Consultant Editor:
DAVID G. CHANDLER
Series Editor: LEE JOHNSON

Produced by DAG Publications Ltd
for Osprey Publishing Ltd.
Colour bird's eye view illustrations b
Cilla Eurich.
Cartography by Micromap.
Wargames consultant Duncan
Macfarlane.
Typeset by Ronset Typesetters,
Darwen, Lancashire.
Mono camerawork by M&E
Reproductions, North Fambridge,
Essex.

▶ *The battlefield of
Waterloo, looking towards
the French position from
the centre of the Anglo-
Netherlands line. The
Charleroi road runs
towards the buildings of
La Belle Alliance, visible
in the background; the
woods of Hougoumont are
the stand of timber in the
right mid-ground,
concealing the château
itself. Early watercolour.
(ASKB)*

11 12 13 14 15   27 26 25 24 23 22 21

The Woodland Trust
Osprey Publishing is supporting the
Woodland Trust, the UK's leading
woodland conservation charity, by
funding the dedication of trees.

www.ospreypublishing.com

Osprey Publishing is part of the
Osprey Group.

Key to
Map Symbols

Army Group	XXXXX ⊠
Army	XXXX ⊠
Corps	XXX ⊠
Division	XX ⊠
Brigade	X ⊠
Cavalry	◨

Printed in China through
World Print Ltd.

Illustration credits. Pictures keyed
'ASKB' are reproduced by
permission of the Anne S. K. Brown
Military Collection

The publishers wish to express their
special gratitude to Philip J.
Haythornthwaite for his expert
assistance in the preparation of this
volume.

CONTENTS

◀ Napoleon's departure from Elba at the beginning of his attempt to regain his throne, on the evening of 26 February 1815; his barge, crewed by Seamen of the Imperial Guard, awaits to row him to his ship Inconstant. (Painting by J. Beaume).

◀ Napoleon aboard his ship Inconstant, returning from Elba to land in France to reclaim his throne, 26 February to 1 March 1815. In addition to his staff, Grenadiers of the 'Elba Battalion' are shown on deck. Painting by Jules Vernet. (ASKB)

◀ Napoleon supervises the landing of his troops from Elba at Golfe Juan, near Antibes, 1 March 1815. The 'Elba Battalion' disembarking at left wears the uniforms of the Grenadiers and Chasseurs à Pied of the Imperial Guard. Print after Friedrich Philip Reinhold. (ASKB)

THE ROAD TO 1815

The early zeal of the French revolutionary armies had been honed over time into a formidable weapon, grasped firmly in the hand of one man – Napoleon Bonaparte. He had not hesitated to wield it in the pursuit of national and personal ends, and the perceived glory of France and her republic. By 1814, however, from his apparent pinnacle of success at Tilsit, the myth of Napoleonic invincibility had been totally shattered. Other countries had gained confidence by copying his methods of organization and tactics, while Russia had finally proved what could be done by sticking it out to the bitter end, costing the Emperor more than 400,000 men in the process. Two years after the devastating catastrophe of the Russian Campaign, France had been bled white by a struggle against overwhelming odds. With a coalition that finally worked (just), the irresistible forces of Austria, Russia, Prussia and other states had finally pressed into the very heart of France itself. French allies such as Bavaria and Saxony had either defected or been overrun, leaving the much reduced French conscript army alone against overwhelming odds. The Allies were content to fight battles of attrition against these numerically inferior and irreplaceable armies, pressing Napoleon back to the very gates of Paris. His political control of France was diluted with every military reverse, and soon the marshals were in revolt. Some defected. With the Allies in Paris, Napoleon was finally persuaded to abdicate in April 1814.

From Empire to Exile

His punishment was to be banishment. The shock was absolute, and at Fontainebleau Napoleon drank the vial of poison he had always carried with him since narrowly avoiding capture in Russia. But although the poison made him gravely ill, it's efficacy had diminished over time, and by 14 April he was well enough to take his leave from his beloved Imperial Guard in a moving scene that touched all hearts. Clad in a general's uniform, and his characteristic hat and greatcoat, he took a tearful farewell, weeping into the colours of the Guard before entering the carriage that was to bear him away. 'Adieu mes enfants! Mes voeux vous accompagneront toujours!'

Travelling in disguise, in fear for his life from the mobs and his enemies, he was transported by coach to the south of France, and beyond to the tiny island of Elba. The terror of the continent, once master of Europe from Lisbon to Moscow, was now lord of a mere islet in the Mediterranean no more than eighteen miles by twelve, his command of the Grande Armée – once around half a million men strong – exchanged for that of a personal guard of just 1,000 men.

Once on Elba, he must have slipped even further into despair. The French government reneged on the two million francs a year income they had promised him, while in Paris his first wife, the Empress Josephine, met an untimely death from diphtheria. Worse was to follow, for his equally beloved second wife, Marie Louise, had been whisked away to the depths of Austria where her impressionable and highly sensual nature quickly allowed her to fall prey to the advances of her new aide-de-camp, General Count Neippberg; and, perhaps worst of all, he was not permitted to see his son, the King of Rome.

To add insult to injury, many of Napoleon's former marshals were using the very wealth and titles he had bestowed on them to entertain in lavish style the very enemies who had caused his downfall. Even Josephine had unashamedly entertained Tsar Alexander in Paris.

Penned on the tiny island, Napoleon moved around restlessly, repeatedly changing his residence, frustrated at his confinement and quickly bored by the mind-numbing routine of Elba, the monotony of the day broken only by meals and card games. The venal Prince de Talleyrand, who had helped to engineer Napoleon's final downfall in Paris, had his spies everywhere, so many that they sometimes spied on each other by mistake. They irritatingly dogged Napoleon's footsteps and fabricated wild and outrageous reports that Talleyrand lost no time in printing in the Bourbon press.

After an initial burst of reforming energy, Napoleon basically ran out of things to do on Elba. His lifestyle became increasingly sedentary, his brilliant mind untaxed. The high spots of his life now came from the snippets of news that slipped in from France, and which must have been his only consolation, since things were not going at all well for the new Bourbon king, Louis XVIII. The welcome relief from war initially felt by the French at the return of the Bourbons soon gave way to great dissatisfaction as the old Bourbon hangers-on flooded back from exile to make their unwelcome mark on the nation and manipulate the system for their own ends. Meanwhile, as the newly crowned Louis lavishly spent the fast-shrinking sixty million francs of Napoleon's amassed treasure, veterans of the wars who had given their youth and health for the nation were left to suffer on hard times. The violet – adopted symbol of the Bonapartists – was soon to be seen discreetly worn in ladies' hair, or in men's lapels.

Meanwhile, the coalition of France's enemies barely lasted to the end of the war. Petty squabbles and in-fighting soon broke out among the Allies at the Congress of Vienna as they jostled for national advantage and swapped minor states like small change in the reorganization of Europe. The united front had broken down, and the minor states were disaffected. Also at Vienna was Talleyrand, who lost no opportunity to stir things up further, demanding that Napoleon be transported well away from Europe to the Azores, or worse. The West Indies and St. Helena were both also proposed, and by the end of 1814 Napoleon knew that Britain and Prussia had agreed in principle to move him, and that Russia's silent acquiescence made it only a matter of time before Napoleon was to lose even Elba.

The unrest in France showed that a small window of opportunity for Napoleon was opening.

Decisive action could perhaps unite the French nation again and restore her pride and glory. Napoleon had little to lose. Ever the opportunist, with the governor of Elba absent in Italy, on 1 March 1815 Napoleon landed in the south of France for perhaps the most famous hundred days in history.

Return of the Emperor

A deliberately slow route to Paris via Nice and Grenoble gave Napoleon time to rebuild and extend his popular support within France. His trickle of followers at Nice became a flood by Grenoble, a veritable torrent of popular support by Lyons. Whole armies sent to capture him deserted to his charismatic appeal, and without firing a shot he entered Paris in triumph on the 20th.

However, in spite of the emotional popular support that was still building in France, he was still far from secure in his position. The all-too-recent horrors of war were not yet forgotten. Bereaved mothers still grieved for their lost sons, wives for their dead husbands; and with the Allies still looking over their shoulders from Vienna, the Chamber of Deputies itself remained cautious and unconvinced. Rumblings in the pro-Bourbon areas of France erupted into uprisings in the Vendee, during March and were to be quashed only in June. Napoleon clearly no longer had the total sovereign authority of previous years. Something had to be done quickly if he were not to lose the momentum he had already built up since his return to France.

Throughout his career he had never been slow to adopt a military solution to international problems, but now he needed time to stabilize the situation. His immediate political overtures were in fact aimed at peace in Europe, with generous terms for the Allies. Nevertheless he prepared to mobilize his forces, and the Allies played right into his hands. Even before he had reached Paris, the Allies had with uncharacteristic consensus put their differences aside and declared war on him on 25 March, together pledging 600,000 men to ensure his final downfall. The rejection of his peace terms in mid-April gave Napoleon the moral justification he needed to begin his campaign. In

▲*At Grenoble on 7 March 1815, Napoleon was confronted by a battalion of the 5th Ligne, intended to arrest him. At the sight of the Emperor they forgot their allegiance to the Bourbon monarchy and flocked to his standard. 'Before Grenoble I was an adventurer', Napoleon remarked; 'after, I was a prince'. (Print after Charles Steuben)*

the face of invasion once again, the French population prepared for war amid a hubbub of activity and excitement.

A swift victory would confirm Napoleon's political position within the country beyond doubt, reinforce his military reputation and offer a strong warning to his enemies to make peace or suffer the consequences of another terrible war. Even a modest success could perhaps shatter the coalition against him. To have any chance of success, he must defeat the Allied armies in detail, before they could converge into an overwhelming force.

Time was clearly of the essence from a military viewpoint, as out of the five armies mobilizing against him, only those of Blücher and Wellington were deployed within striking distance of France by late May, and even these were spread thinly over a wide area – offering Napoleon the possibility of surprise attacks with local superiority. As a bonus, defeating the unbeaten Wellington could conceivably bring the UK stock market crashing down, and with it the British Government, taking a highly indebted Britain out of the conflict for months to come.

Further, by defeating Blücher and Wellington and taking control of the Low Countries, Napoleon would be following the tried and tested Revolutionary Wars principle of exporting trouble at home to a neighbouring country. He would also immediately boost his available manpower from these largely pro-French countries and provide encouragement to the German and Polish states to once again join with him before the war was taken to their lands with the arrival of the Austrian and Russian armies. Already, mutiny in the Prussian army had caused 14,000 discontented Saxons to be sent home.

THE OPPOSING COMMANDERS

The French Commanders

Napoleon stands as one of the greatest commanders of all time, with a reputation that even today holds military leaders in awe. Probably only Alexander the Great can match his laurels on the field of battle, with perhaps the added edge that can only go to those commanders who die young; for by the campaign of 1815, although still highly talented, superbly charismatic and strategically brilliant when on form, this was not really the Napoleon of the Italian or Danubian campaigns. Aged 46 at the time of Waterloo, he was not a well man. Years of soft living interspersed with the rigours and long hours of campaign had taken their toll, as had the eleven indolent months in Elban

Napoleon in 1815, wearing his famous grey greatcoat (Print after Paul Delaroche)

exile. This was not the tireless figure of Austerlitz, immediately present wherever crisis loomed, rushing to centre or to flank to bolster morale and issue orders. Even riding a horse now caused him severe physical discomfort, and it has been suggested that his haemorrhoids had reappeared during his exile in Elba. The evidence is not conclusive, but certainly Napoleon had suffered from this malady as a younger man.

He was also possibly suffering from acromegaly, a glandular disorder that makes one subject to intermittent bouts of both torpor and over-optimism. We will see evidence of what may well be these symptoms in Napoleon's performance during the campaign. His lessened attention to detail, periods of mental weariness, unjustified over-optimism and diminished drive – highly symptomatic of the disease – all contributed to his overall lack of success in 1815. His stamina after Elba was much lowered, and it was to desert him on more than one occasion in this campaign. The impact was that the intense, almost absolute unity of purpose that once characterized his way of waging war was now diluted, and both of his opposing generals were able to recover from mistakes and avoid disaster in the Waterloo campaign because of it. Generals did not usually get a second chance when they were facing Bonaparte.

On the battlefield, although his reputation was still formidable, the earlier intense energy, genius and the finesse of the enveloping battlefield manoeuvre seen at, for example, Castiglione, Ulm, Austerlitz and Jena had now gone. Whereas in 1805 it could be said: 'The Emperor has discovered a new way of waging war; he makes us use our legs instead of our arms', this innovative approach had been eroded over the years in favour of the large-scale, bloody, hard-fought frontal assaults seen at Wagram, Borodino, Leipzig – and now to be repeated at Ligny and Mont St. Jean. A frontal assault is a battle of attrition, rather than manoeuvre. Although brutal, it is quick to set up and execute, takes less concentration and energy on the part of the commander and can be supervised more easily than a battle of manoeuvre. Napoleon's most decisive victories had been his early ones – all battles of manoeuvre followed by vigorous pursuit. His increasing dependence in his later battles on frontal assaults (from about Wagram onwards) probably suggests tactical decline and over-optimism. This dangerous habit of underestimating the strength and capabilities of one's enemy can influence considerably the outcome of a campaign, and it is perhaps interesting to observe that although by 1815 Napoleon had never really lost a battle when he was present on the field, he also never won a campaign outright after 1809. Certainly, unlike the Napoleon of Austerlitz, we see him now increasingly content to allow tactical control on the day to pass to a battle commander – and at Waterloo the choice of Marshal Ney for this role was to be far-reaching.

In 1815, Napoleon was still a great commander, with a genius for strategy that was easily to outmatch Wellington and Blücher in this campaign. On form, he had a sparkle and insight that can only be described as breathtaking; but his form was to vary wildly and unpredictably during the Waterloo campaign, along with his energy. Of all the commanders of the period, he had a unique ability to inspire the rank and file to incredible feats of bravery and determination – even today he inspires from the grave – but tactically, Wellington was markedly his better, obtaining inspired results in spite of regular shortages in cavalry and artillery, and often with poorer raw material within his armies.

Given the sometimes variable qualities of the Emperor in 1815, the quality of the staff supporting him would be crucial to the eventual success of the campaign; but in the choice of key staff officers there was a lot to be desired. Napoleon personally appointed his staff, and difficulties and mistakes here show the real importance of good leadership. Many of the blunders and errors that later dogged the campaign for the French came from the choices made here, many of whom were appointed for political reasons. In choosing his staff, Napoleon either failed or refused to play to their strengths, perhaps counting on his own bright but fading genius to overcome the deficiencies inherent in his command, and hoping to reap all the credit.

Admittedly, the obvious choice for Chief of Staff, Berthier, was no longer available to him, for he had crashed to his death from a high window early in June 1815. Napoleon and Berthier had made an excellent team during many campaigns, Berthier having the knack of overcoming detail shortcomings in Napoleon's 'broad brush' concepts and interpreting his general ideas and rather poor Corsican French (and appalling handwriting) into practical operations. In Berthier's absence, the logical choice for Chief of Staff was Marshal Louis-Gabriel Suchet, an extremely able, experienced and competent choice for this demanding and critical position. But perhaps Suchet would have been too good a choice for Napoleon, who had always operated his generals on a 'divide and rule' principle and rarely exposed to the world a rival for the laurels of victory. Whatever the reason, this able commander found himself posted to Lyons, well away from any position of influence in the coming campaign.

Instead, Marshal Nicolas Jean de Dieu Soult was made Chief of Staff, a position for which he had relatively little prior experience, and unproven ability. Many of the communication problems during the campaign can be laid at his door, with key orders written ambivalently, misplaced, or sent late. As one of Napoleon's best and most experienced field officers, Soult should have been in command of the left wing of the army against Wellington, who was tactically almost certainly the best army commander in Europe by 1815. Soult had fought Wellington in the Peninsula and the Pyrenees, and well knew his temperament and wily ways of fighting.

Instead, the left wing of the army went to Marshal Michel Ney, a choice that was ultimately to prove fatal. This officer had almost manic tendencies, and was quite possibly suffering from battle fatigue. Periods of intense, impetuous, almost irrational activity were interspersed with periods of total caution, lethargy and inactivity.

▲ Marshal Michel Ney, prince de la Moskowa, duc d'Elchingen (1769-1815); known as 'the bravest of the brave', he was Napoleon's chief subordinate in the Hundred Days campaign. He has been criticized for his conduct at Quatre Bras and Waterloo. (Engraving by R. G. Tietze after François Gérard)

▲ Marshal Emmanuel, Marquis de Grouchy (1766-1847); a skilled cavalry commander, but perhaps unsuited for the task of leading Napoleon's right wing in the Waterloo campaign. (Engraving by Henry Wolf after Jean-Sébastien Rouillard)

Even by Napoleon's own assessment, Ney's ability to think strategically was extremely limited, and on more than one occasion he had compromised Napoleon's plans by rash action. Yet this officer was given command of the left wing, a wing planned to be semi-independent if Napoleon turned his attention to deal with the Prussians. It required both energy and perception to take key objectives and prevent the Allies uniting, and being required to exploit any strategic opportunities that a slow British mobilization could present.

On the other hand, it did show politically that Napoleon would be prepared to forgive and forget as regards Bourbon generals – Ney was formerly Commander-in-Chief of the Bourbon forces and had promised Louis that he would bring Napoleon back in an iron cage. Ney also had great charisma and popularity with the rank and file.

The right wing of the army went to Marshal Emmanuel de Grouchy, an expert cavalry commander who was totally inexperienced at handling large forces of combined arms in a Senior Command capacity. Grouchy would have been an obvious choice for command of the Cavalry reserve, given Napoleon's refusal to employ Murat – probably the greatest cavalry commander in Europe – who had defected to the Allies in 1814. Grouchy had in fact only just received his marshal's baton – the 26th, and last, of the Emperor's Marshals.

The best choice for the right wing – against the Prussians – would have clearly been Marshal

Louis-Nicolas Davout. He had beaten the Prussians on numerous occasions, and they showed him a healthy respect and caution. His tremendous ability had made him seem the only serious rival to Napoleon in the early years of the Empire, but although this honourable, apolitical and talented soldier gave unquestioning loyalty to Napoleon throughout his imperial career, perhaps the Corsican mind could never quite put the early days aside. The suspicion that Napoleon would have to share the laurels once again reared its head, and, with the political stability of Napoleon's regime far from assured, Davout – Napoleon's undefeated marshal – was left in Paris as Minister of War – well away from the action.

The few hours that Napoleon took to select his staff arguably had as much impact on the eventual outcome of the campaign as the combined efforts of more than 220,000 Allied troops between 15 and 18 June, as will be seen.

In sum, although past his very best, Napoleon was still among the world's great leaders in 1815, but supported by a staff that was less than perfect for the task ahead of it. Deficiencies would therefore have to be compensated by the dogged performance of the rank and file, and Napoleon's ability to inspire them would be the key to this. It was a facility he possessed above all others: his men would literally risk death for a friendly tug on the ear from their Emperor, and Wellington put it very succinctly when he declared that on the field of battle the sight of his hat was worth 40,000 men.

The British Commanders

Wellington was the same age as Napoleon. Born with the family name of Wellesley, he was the third son of an Anglo-Irish peer, and as such had to find himself a career. After an indifferent schooling at Eton, he more or less drifted into the army in a manner not untypical of his day. The British purchase system ensured his rapid promotion as he moved from regiment to regiment until by 1794 he was in command of the 33rd Foot, with whom he joined the retreating army of the Duke of York during the Flanders campaign, the 33rd distinguishing itself at the Dommel.

The campaign in Flanders was a disaster, and

▲ *Field Marshal Arthur Wellesley, 1st Duke of Wellington (1769-1852), commander of the Anglo-Netherlands forces. (Painting by Sir Thomas Lawrence)*

it made an impression that was to help develop his philosophy for the British army in his later years. As he later recalled: 'I learnt more by seeing our own faults and the defects of our system in the campaign of Holland than anywhere else. The Regiments were as good in proper hands as they are now, but the system was wretched.' The system was indeed wretched, for although in Wellington it produced a first-class general, this was the exception rather than the rule, and capable senior officers were very thin on the ground. Furthermore, the commissariat was so corrupt that the Royal Wagon Corps soon earned itself the nickname of 'The Newgate Blues'. 'I learned what not to do,' he said 'and that is always something.'

It was India that shaped his skill on the

battlefield. He spent eight years there, following his elder brother who had been made Governor General in 1798. Wellesley quickly rose to the rank of Major-General, and was the victor of the Mahratta War, with many successes to his credit. But these counted for little within the career-officer culture that met him upon his return. He was branded a 'sepoy general', an outrageous slur given the almost total lack of active fighting experience in British officers at the time.

It was in Spain and Portugal that he really made his name, working with Britain's Iberian allies to develop an army that gradually cleared the peninsula of French troops and entered France itself. When the armistice was signed in 1814, the Duke of Wellington (as he was by now) had not faced an army led by Napoleon himself; only now, in 1815, were the two great generals destined to meet on the field of battle.

In personality, temperament and outlook the two men were as different as chalk and cheese. Where Napoleon inspired by sheer charisma, tempered by volatile outbursts, Wellington led by cool ability and competence. While Napoleon elevated strategy to an almost intuitive art form, Wellington developed a style that depended on analysis and logic. Where Napoleon would throw troops in by the thousand, sometimes wastefully, Wellington would hoard his meagre army and begrudge improvident loss of human life. A hard, aloof, but always fair man, Wellington set both his officers and himself intolerably high standards. A thorough aristocrat, he despised the raw material from the classes that typically made up the rank and file; but he had total respect for the quality of the fighting men his system produced and would set them – the infantry at least – against any foe.

In this campaign at least, the vagaries of the British appointments system provided him with what was on the whole to be a good British command – almost by accident it seems, for Wellington was not pleased with the staff that awaited him upon his taking command. Although he was able to make some key changes, including appointing the very able Sir William Delancey as Quartermaster General, the remainder of his command proved very much of mixed quality. Although many of the officers he would have

wanted (such as Alexander Dickson, who would have commanded the artillery) were *en route* from America, in some respects it was a well-tried team. Some of his senior officers, such as General Sir Roland 'Daddy' Hill were highly respected, having served with him in Spain; others were inexperienced but confident; and as for the others, he made do with what he had.

The 22-year-old Prince of Orange, for example, was very inexperienced, but at the time war was declared was in command of the 30,000 or so native Dutch/Belgian troops. It was with reluctance that he handed over command to Wellington, and only the infantry at that until the very morning of Waterloo itself. In the very nick of time too, for 'The Young Frog' (as he was known in the British ranks) was about to launch an uncoordinated, unsupported and almost certainly doomed offensive against Napoleon on his own initiative. For political reasons he received I Corps.

Another interesting appointment was that of the Earl of Uxbridge as both Wellington's second-in-command and commander of the cavalry. He was appointed against Wellington's express wishes. Professionally, Uxbridge was a very able officer, but he was not on the best of personal terms with Wellington, for there was deep scandal in the family – Uxbridge had eloped with Wellington's sister-in-law. Wellington was to treat Uxbridge with cool politeness during the campaign. Certainly Uxbridge was not privy to his commander's inner thoughts, and when he tactfully asked Wellington what his plans were, in case anything untoward were to occur to his person, all he received was the icy reply, 'My plans, Sir, are to beat the French'.

If the higher echelons of the Allied force were of variable quality, it was fortunate for Wellington that at divisional level his command was both competent and reliable; officers such as Picton, Maitland, Cooke and Ompteda were to repay Wellington's trust in them. It would be unfair, however, not to recognize also the abilities of many of his Netherlands commanders, most of whom had served under French command in the preceding campaigns. For example, the benefits of their French training were to be demonstrated by Perponcher and Saxe-Weimar at Quatre Bras,

◀ *Prince William of Orange (1792-1849), later King William II of the Netherlands distributing medals; commander of the Anglo-Netherlands I Corps, he was nominally Wellington's deputy despite being dangerously inexperienced. (Print published by Thomas Kelly)*

▲ *Henry William Paget, Earl of Uxbridge (1768–1854) who commanded the Allied cavalry at Waterloo and was to lose a leg during the battle. He became the first Marquess of Anglesey in 1815. (Engraving after the portrait by Sir Thomas Lawrence.)*

▲*Field Marshal Gebhard Leberecht von Blücher, Prince of Wahlstadt (1742-1819), commander of the* *Prussian army. (Engraving by T. W. Harland after F. C. Gröger)*

▲*General August Wilhelm Anton, Count Neithardt von Gneisenau (1760-1831); Blücher's* *Chief-of-Staff. (Portrait by P. E. Gebauer)*

where bold initiative and intelligence – the hallmark of the French approach – were to be critical to Wellington's survival and eventual success.

Prince Wahlstadt Gebhard von Blücher

In spite of the fact that he was more than 72 years old in 1815, Blücher retained a fiery energy and an indomitable courage. A blustering hussar mentality encouraged him to lead from the front, which inspired his men but afforded him a narrow view of the battlefield not always conducive to victory. In his later career his partnership with General Graf Niethard von Gneisenau contributed greatly to his successes, Blücher providing the determination and inspiration, Gneisenau the brainwork.

Blücher had fought both *against* the Prussians in the Seven Years War and *for* them (which was not unusual in those days of the professional gentleman soldier). Blücher's fiery passions for

gambling, wenching and drinking did not exactly further his military career, and, following a quarrel with Frederick the Great, he spent sixteen years in 'retirement' in Silesia before returning to the colours once more with the accession of Frederick Wilhelm III. He had risen to the rank of lieutenant-general by 1806, when he was captured after the Battles of Jena and Auerstadt – which battles Blücher sought to avenge right up to 1815, gaining many successes in Silesia during the 1813 campaigns. His capture perhaps contributed to his great personal hatred of Napoleon, and his desire to capture and hang him was to be a key motivation during the 1815 campaign along with a genuine love of his troops and a great sense of patriotism. Honour and loyalty were perhaps his two principle qualities, and without them Wellington would have lost the Battle of Waterloo – the contribution of the anglophobic Gneisenau, alone would not have been enough.

OPPOSING ARMIES

L'Armée du Nord

It was certainly Napoleon's charisma that brought thousands of French veterans back to the colours for the campaign, augmenting the hastily conscripted levies to provide a backbone of high-morale troops to the less enthusiastic conscripts who made up substantial parts of the army from May onwards. Many of these veterans found their way into the Imperial Guard for the 1815 campaign, following a slight relaxation in the rules governing eligibility but probably not quality. There was nothing unusual in thus creaming off the veterans, as the Guard traditionally took some

of the best troops from the line regiments, training them for junior and intermediate rank leadership roles before returning them to the line regiments in a command capacity. This had the advantage of providing an example for the raw recruits in their charge and maintaining high standards and expectations within the rank and file. However, the peace of 1814 had broken the rhythm of this system, and in 1815 the veterans were hoarded

▼'Inspection': Napoleon and the Grenadiers à Pied of the Imperial Guard, here in their dress uniform (overall trousers were generally worn on campaign). Lithograph by Auguste Raffet. (ASKB)

carefully within the Guard at the expense of the line regiments.

Even by hoarding troops, however, numbers in the Guard did not achieve the figures for previous campaigns: compared with the 112,480 men of the 1814 campaign, Waterloo was to see an Imperial Guard of 25,000. The 4th Grenadiers of the Middle Guard, for example, found themselves able to muster only a single battalion.

If numbers were comparatively tight in the Guard, what of the rest of the army? On 1 June, Napoleon held a spectacular review – *Le Champ de Mai* – at which he presented Eagles to the troops. One eyewitness, Captain Coignet of the Imperial Guard reveals that 'the Emperor made a speech. He had the eagles brought to him to distribute to the army and the national guard. With that stentorian voice of his, he cried to them, "Swear to defend your eagles! Do you swear it?," he repeated. But the vows were made without warmth; there was but little enthusiasm: the shouts were not like those of Austerlitz and Wagram, and the Emperor perceived it . . .' Maybe this view reflects more of the élitist nature of a guardsman than the state of the army, or perhaps the pomp and ceremony was out of place in the survivalist mood of 1815, for even his old soldiers were shocked by their Emperor. He had put aside his well known uniform and hat in favour of an embroidered violet mantle of state, crimson velvet

The Young Guard:
1, Private, Voltigeurs,
campaign dress;

2, Officer, Tirailleurs,
campaign dress. (Bryan
Fosten)

▶ 'The Field of May'. Napoleon mounted an impressive parade in Paris on 1 June 1815, to present 'Eagles' to the army and encourage support; but his appearance in state dress rather than the expected military uniform disappointed the onlookers. (Print after F. de Myrbach)

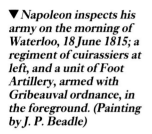

▼ Napoleon inspects his army on the morning of Waterloo, 18 June 1815; a regiment of cuirassiers at left, and a unit of Foot Artillery, armed with Gribeauval ordnance, in the foreground. (Painting by J. P. Beadle)

ORDER OF BATTLE: THE FRENCH ARMY

The Emperor Napoleon

Total strength of the French Army: approx 128,000 men, 366 guns

I Corps

D'Erlon

1st Division (Allix/Quiot)
54th 55th Light Infantry (Quiot)
28th 105th Infantry (Bourgeois)

2nd Division (Donzelot)
13th Light Infantry, 17th Infantry (Schmitz)
19th 31st Infantry (Aulard)

3rd Division (Marcognet)
21st 46th Infantry (Noguez)
25th 45th Infantry (Grenier)

4th Division (Durutte)
8th 29th Infantry (Pegot)
85th 95th Infantry (Brue)

1st Cavalry Division (Jaquinot)
7th Hussars, 3rd Chasseurs (Bruno)
3rd 4th Lancers (Gobrecht)

I Corps Artillery (de Salles)
5 foot batteries
1 horse battery

II Corps

Reille

5th Division (Bachelu)
2nd Light Infantry, 3rd Infantry (Husson)
72nd 108th Infantry (Campi)

6th Division (Jérôme)
1st Light Infantry, 3rd Infantry (Baudouin)
1st 2nd Infantry (Soye)

7th Division (Girard)
11th Light Infantry, 82nd Infantry (Villiers)
12th Light Infantry, 4th Infantry (Piat)

9th Division (Foy)
92nd 93rd Infantry (Gauthier)
4th Light Infantry, 100th Infantry (Jamin)

2nd Cavalry Division (Piré)
1st 6th Chasseurs (Hubert)
5th 6th Lancers (Wathiez)

II Corps Artillery (Pellitier)
5 foot batteries
1 horse battery

III Corps

Vandamme

8th Division (Lefol)
15th Light Infantry, 23rd Infantry (Billiard)
37th 64th Infantry (Corsin)

10th Division (Hubert)
34th 88th Infantry (Gengoult)
22nd 70th Infantry, 2nd (Swiss) Infantry (Dupeyroux)

11th Division (Berthezène)
12th 56th Infantry (Dufour)
33rd 86th Infantry (Lagarde)

3rd Cavalry Division (Domon)
4th 9th Chasseurs (Dommanget)
12th Chasseurs (Vinot)

III Corps Artillery (Douguereau)
4 foot batteries
1 horse battery

IV Corps

Gérard

12th Division (Pêcheux)
30th 96th Infantry (Rome)
6th Light Infantry, 63rd Infantry (Schoeffer)

13th Division (Vichery)
59th 76th Infantry (le Capitaine)
48th 69th Infantry (Desprez)

14th Division (Bourmont/Hulot)
9th Light Infantry, 111th Infantry (Hulot)
44th 50th Infantry (Toussaint)

7th Cavalry Division (Maurin)
6th Hussars, 8th Chasseurs (Vallin)
6th 11th 16th Dragoons (Berruyer)

IV Corps Artillery (Baltus)
4 foot batteries
1 horse battery

VI Corps

Lobau

19th Division (Simmer)
5th 11th Infantry (Bellair)
27th 84th Infantry (Jamin)

20th Division (Jeanin)
5th Light Infantry, 10th Infantry (Bony)
107th Infantry (Tromelin)

21st Division (Teste)
8th Light Infantry (Lafitte)
65th 75th Infantry (Penne)

VI Corps Artillery (Noury)
4 foot batteries
1 horse battery

I Cavalry Corps

Pajol

4th Cavalry Division (Soult)
1st 4th Hussars (St Laurent)
5th Hussars (Ameil)

5th Cavalry Division (Subervie)
1st 2nd Lancers (Colbert)
11th Chasseurs (Douai)
Artillery
2 horse batteries

II Cavalry Corps

Exelmans

9th Cavalry Division (Strolz)
5th 13th Dragoons (Burthe)
15th 20th Dragoons (Vincent)

10th Cavalry Division (Chastel)
4th 12th Dragoons (Bennemains)
14th 17th Dragoons (Berton)
Artillery
2 horse batteries

III Cavalry Corps

Kellermann

11th Cavalry Division (l'Héritier)
2nd 7th Dragoons (Picquet)
8th 11th Cuirassiers (Guiton)

12th Cavalry Division (d'Hurbal)
1st 2nd Carabiniers (Blanchard)
2nd 3rd Cuirassiers (Donop)
Artillery
2 horse batteries

IV Cavalry Corps

Milhaud

13th Cavalry Division (Wathier)
1st 4th Cuirassiers (Dubois)
7th 12th Cuirassiers (Travers)

14th Cavalry Division (Delort)
5th 10th Cuirassiers (Vial)
6th 9th Cuirassiers (Farine)
Artillery
2 horse batteries

tunic, velvet togue with white plume, white satin vest and breeches, white satin shoes with diamond buckles, Grand Cross of the Legion of Honour in diamonds and rubies, and a diamond hilted sword. It was not perhaps the attire a corpulent middle-aged general would usually wear to inspire fanatical emotion in his troops.

In fact, the vast majority of the troops in Napoleon's army of 1815 were volunteers, predominantly with an intense devotion to the Emperor. Many of the line troops had fought in previous campaigns, and the army was based almost entirely on French nationals – in contrast to some of the 1813-14 armies, which had included substantial proportions of sometimes half-hearted and dubious allies. Many of the troops saw themselves as fighting to protect their homeland from invasion once more, and this must have been a significant boost to the motivation of even the newest conscript soldiers.

Smaller this army may have been, hastily trained and ill-equipped it certainly was; but in terms of overall quality it was probably one of the better armies that Napoleon had commanded and certainly one of the most homogeneous. The only real question-mark hung over those troops who until recently had formed the French army under the Bourbons. These formed part of the right wing under Grouchy's command and were treated with utmost suspicion and near contempt by their peers during the Hundred Days.

So, amazing as it now seems, from leaving Elba with almost nothing, Napoleon managed to put 128,000 good-quality men into the field in a matter of months. With essential military equipment either improvised or scraped together from all available sources, Napoleon crossed the Belgian frontier early on 15 June with his 'Armée du Nord' to take on the Allies who had so recently bayed for his abdication. He was convinced that he would soon make short work of the Prussians again, and would show the world that Wellington's reputation was seriously over-rated. Had he understood Wellington and Blücher a little better, perhaps he would not have been quite so confident.

Wellington's Army

Of the two Allied armies, the Anglo-Allied army was the least homogeneous. Described by Wellington as an 'infamous' army, it consisted of a polyglot of British, German, Hanoverian, Brunswick, Nassau and Dutch-Belgian troops. Of these the British and King's German Legion were the most dependable, but many of Wellington's Peninsula veterans were away fighting in America, leaving well-trained but untried and unproven troops in their place. The famous 2nd Royal North British Dragoons (Scots Greys), for example, had not seen active service as a unit since 1801! Overall, however, the British soldier was to acquit himself well, and the British contingents were the

---

Imperial Guard

Drouot (Mortier absent)

Grenadier Division (Friant)	**Guard Heavy Cavalry Division**
1st 2nd Grenadiers (Friant)	**(Guyot)**
3rd 4th Grenadiers (Rouguet)	Grenadiers à Cheval (Jamin)
	Guard Dragoons (Letort)
Chasseur Division (Morand)	Gendarmerie d'Elite (Dyonnet)
1st 2nd Chasseurs (Morand)	
2nd 3rd Chasseurs (Michel)	**Guard Artillery**
	(Deployed with Guard infantry and cavalry)
Young Guard (Duhesme)	6 medium foot batteries
1st Tirailleurs 1st Voltigeurs (Chartrand)	4 horse batteries
3rd Tirailleurs 3rd Voltigeurs (Guye)	
	Guard Artillery Reserve
Guard Light Cavalry Division	**(Desvaux de Saint-Maurice)**
(Lefebvre-Desnouëttes)	4 heavy foot batteries
Guard Chasseurs à Cheval (Lallemand)	
Lancers of the Guard (Colbert-Chabanais)	

▼ *1, Sergeant-major, 33rd (1st Yorkshire, West Riding) Regiment; 2, Private, 69th (South Lincolnshire) Regiment; 3, Adjutant, 54th (West Norfolk) Regiment. (Bryan Fosten)*

keystones of Wellington's divisions. The kilted Highlanders were particularly terrifying, to foe and ally alike, the skirl of the pipes and terrifying screams that accompanied their ferocious charge justly earning them the nickname of 'ladies from hell'.

The Kings German Legion (KGL) were German troops clothed in British style uniforms, trained by Britain and incorporated into Wellington's command. They were highly experienced troops of superb quality and brilliant leadership. In the KGL alone, a foreign force in British service, was promotion within Wellington's army possible primarily on merit rather than by purchase, demonstrating what British training could do with genuine talent.

Alas, many of the Hanoverian units, although similarly clothed in British uniforms, were of decidedly conscript quality. Wellington sprinkled these among his veterans to provide them with some suitable bolstering and to minimize desertion. Wherever possible, Wellington's tactic was to place these troops in the second line.

Of the rest, the tiny contingent of Nassauers were also fine troops, and the black Brunswickers

provided a useful if inexperienced force of very young troops; but it was the Dutch-Belgians who gave Wellington most cause for concern. Making up almost 30 per cent of Wellington's command, until very recently they had been allied to the French, and their leanings – especially those of the Belgian troops – were still very much in this direction. Even their uniforms and equipment followed the French pattern, as did their columnar tactics and formations. With such motivation, and the youthful and inexperienced Prince of Orange providing dubious leadership, it would be unfair not to make some allowances for the overall mixed, but by no means poor, performance of these troops during the campaign.

The Anglo-Allies were organized into a Cavalry Corps, two main Infantry Corps and a Reserve.

▼*Assembly of the 2nd (Coldstream) Foot Guards on the morning of Waterloo, depicting the service uniform of the British infantry, here with the shoulder-wings of a flank company. The 2nd Battalion 2nd Guards* *served in Byng's British 2nd Brigade, and assisted in the defence of Hougoumont. (Print after James Thiriar)*

ORDER OF BATTLE: THE ANGLO-ALLIED ARMY

Field Marshal The Duke of Wellington

Total strength of the Anglo-Allied Army: approx 106,000 men, 216 cannon, including garrisons

I Corps

The Prince of Orange

1st Division (Cooke)
2/1st 3/1st Guards (Maitland)
2/2nd 2/3rd Guards (Byng)
Artillery (Adye)
 Sandham's Field Brigade R. A.
 Kühlmann's Horse Artillery KGL

3rd Division (Alten)
2/30th 33rd 2/69th 2/73rd (Colin Halkett)
1st 2nd Light Btns KGL, 5th 8th Line KGL (Ompteda)
6 Battalions Hanoverians (Kielmansegge)
Artillery (Williamson)
 Lloyd's Field Brigade R. A.
 Cleeve's Field Brigade KGL

2nd Dutch Belgian Division (Perponcher)
7th Line, 27th Jäger, 5th 7th 8th Militia (Bylandt)
2nd Nassau Regiment of Orange Nassau (Saxe-Weimar)
Artillery (Opstal)
 Byleveld's Horse Artillery
 Stievenaar's Foot Artillery

3rd Dutch Belgian Division (Chassé)
2nd Line, 35th Jäger, 4th 6th 17th 19th Militia (Ditmers)
3rd 12th 13th Line, 36th Jäger, 3rd 10th Militia (d'Aubremé)
Artillery (van der Smissen)
 Krahmer's Horse Battery
 Lux's Foot Battery

II Corps

Lord Hill

2nd Division (Clinton)
1/52nd 1/71st 2/95th 3/95th (Adam)
1st 2nd 3rd 4th Line Btns KGL (du Plat)
4 Hanoverian Landwehr Bns (H. Halkett)
Artillery (Gold)
 Bolton's Battery R. A.
 Sympher's Horse Battery KGL

4th Division (Colville)
3/14th 1/23rd 51st (Mitchell)
2/35th 1/54th 2/59th 1/91st (Johnstone)
2 Hanoverian Line Bns, 3 Landwehr (Lyon)
Artillery (Hawker)
 Brome's Battery R. A.
 Rettburg's Hanoverian Foot Artillery

1st Dutch Belgian Division (Stedmann)
4th 6th Line, 16th Jäger, 9th 14th 15th Militia (Hauw)
1st Line, 18th Jäger, 1st 2nd 18th Militia (Eerens)
Artillery
 Wynand's Foot Artillery
4 Bns, 1 Field Battery (Netherland's Indian Brigade)

Cavalry Corps

Uxbridge

1st 2nd Life Guards, Royal Horse Guards,
1st Dragoon Guards (Somerset)
1st Royal Dragoons, 2nd North British Dragoons,
6th Inniskilling Dragoons (Ponsonby)
1st 2nd Light Dragoons KGL, 23rd Light Dragoons (Dörnberg)
11th 12th 16th Light Dragoons (Vandeleur)
7th 15th Hussars, 2nd Hussars KGL (Grant)
10th 18th Hussars, 1st Hussars KGL (Vivian)
13th Light Dragoons KGL, 3rd Hussars KGL (Arentschildt)
Attached Artillery (Fraser)
 Bull's Troop R. H. A.
 Webber-Smith's R. H. A.
 Gardiner's R. H. A.
 Whinyate's R. H. A.
 Ramsay's R. H. A.
 Mercer's R. H. A.
Prince Regents Hussars, Bremen and Verden Hussars,
Duke of Cumberland's Hussars (Estorff)
1st 3rd Dutch Carabiniers, 2nd Belgian Carabiniers (Trip)
4th Dutch Light Dragoons, 8th Belgian Hussars (Ghingy)
5th Belgian Light Dragoons, 6th Dutch Hussars (Merlen)
Artillery
 Two half horse batteries
Cavalry of the Brunswick Corps
 Regt Hussars, Regt Uhlans

Reserve

under command of the Duke of Wellington

5th Division (Picton)
1/28th 1/32nd 1/79th 1/95th (Kempt)
3/1st 1/42nd 2/44th 1/92nd (Pack)
4 Hanoverian Landwehr Bns (Vincke)
Artillery (Heisse)
 Roger's R. A.
 Braun's Hanoverian Foot Artillery

6th Division (Cole)
1/4th 1/27th 1/40th 2/81st (Lambert)
4 Hanoverian Landwehr Bns (Best)
Artillery (Bruckmann)
 Unett's R. A.
 Sinclair's R. A.

British Reserve Artillery (Drummond)
Ross' R. H. A.
Bean's R. H. A.
Morrison's R. A.
Hutchesson's R. A.
Ibert's R. A.

Brunswick Corps (The Duke of Brunswick)
Brunswick Advance Guard (Rauschenplatt)
Guard Btn, 1st 2nd 3rd Light (Buttlar)
1st 2nd 3rd Line Bns (Specht)
Artillery (Mahn)
 Heinemann's Horse Battery
 Moll's Foot Battery

Hanoverian Reserve Corps (Decken)
12 Hanoverian Bns in Garrisons

▲Two of the regiments especially distinguished at Waterloo: the 92nd (Gordon) Highlanders (Sir Denis Pack's 9th British Brigade, Picton's 5th Division) and (in the bearskin caps) the 2nd (Royal North British) Dragoons (Royal Scots Greys). They are

portrayed here by Johann Georg Paul Fischer in 1814, but have substantially the costume worn at Waterloo; the sporrans, however, were not worn on campaign. (ASKB)

These were deployed in the area between Brussels, Mons, Ypres and Ghent, with lines of communication going back to Ostend and the Channel ports. Thus a French sweep towards the coast could give Wellington severe supply problems. In fact, Wellington was particularly sensitive, perhaps excessively so, to a possible threat to his communications. He was to keep substantial parts of his army placed at Mons to cover his communications until almost the last minute.

Blücher's Army

The Prussians had reorganized on the French model after the disaster of 1806, and although the size of their standing army had initially been limited, they had introduced a system of reservists to make ultimate remobilization a quicker process. There were no guard units present during the 1815 campaign, and the qualitative backbone of this Prussian army lay in the original twelve, long-established 'old' regiments (36 battalions) and, to a lesser extent, the twelve reservist regiments.

During 1814/15 Prussia had also levied large numbers of new troops from the provinces to make up the required numbers. To that end, much of the revitalized Prussian army – over half of it – was of 'Landwehr' status, hastily and poorly equipped, lacking in discipline and experience, but in some cases fighting as a patriotic force for their revered Blücher. Indeed, although the term 'Prussian army' is used, this was not a homogeneous force. Significant reorganization may have increased the size of the Prussian army, but it had also brought in, besides the novice Landwehr, troops from newly acquired provinces whose loyalty was not unquestioned. Mass desertions from the veteran Russo-German Legion had occurred as early as 1814, for example, as state boundaries had changed, and the 10,000 troops from what had recently been the Confederation of the Rhine states deserted at the first reverse (Ligny). The

Saxons and Silesians – 14,000 strong – did not even last that long, but were disarmed after mutiny before the campaign opened. Even some of the more Germanic states – such as Westphalia – were unreliable. With more time, greater cohesion could have followed, but time was a luxury Napoleon was not to allow them. Troops from newly acquired states were therefore mixed into corps with the more reliable Prussian troops to stiffen their performance – with variable success.

Given the static and limited numbers of experienced and trustworthy officers, the infantry corps were thus large and of mixed quality. As might be expected from such large organizations, at corps level the Prussian infantry was a big but rather blunt and unwieldy weapon. Overwhelming numbers were seen to be the secret of success, rather than fine tactics.

The cavalry had suffered from reorganizations that had lumped together regiments of different weapon and training types and from different provinces, many of which were new acquisitions of the Prussian state. The scarcity of horses in eastern Europe was a real problem, and many

ORDER OF BATTLE
THE PRUSSIAN ARMY

Field Marshal Gebhard Leberecht von Blücher, Prince of Wahlstadt

Total strength of the Prussian Army: approx 128,000 men, 312 guns, including garrisons

I Corps

von Ziethen

12th 24th Infantry, 1st Westphalian Landwehr (Steinmetz)
6th 28th Infantry, 2nd Westphalian Landwehr (Pirch II)
7th 29th Infantry, 3rd Westphalian Landwehr (Jagow)
19th Infantry, 4th Westphalian Landwehr (Donnersmarck)
I Corps Cavalry (Röder)
  2nd 5th Dragoons, Brandenburg Uhlans (Treskow)
  6th Uhlans, 1st 2nd Kurmark Landwehr, 1st Silesian Hussars,
  1st Westphalian Landwehr (Lützow)
I Corps Artillery (Lehmann)
  3 horse batteries
  3 12pdr field batteries
  5 6pdr field batteries
  1 Howitzer battery

II Corps

Pirch I

2nd 25th Infantry, 5th Westphalian Landwehr (Tippelskirch)
9th 26th Infantry, 1st Elbe Landwehr (Kraft)
14th 22nd Infantry, 2nd Elbe Landwehr (Brause)
21st 23rd Infantry, 3rd Elbe Landwehr (Bose)
II Corps Cavalry (Wahlen-Jürgass)
  Silesian Uhlans, 6th Dragoons, 11th Hussars (Thümen)
  1st Dragoons, 4th Kurmark Landwehr (Schulenburg)
  3rd 5th Hussars, 5th Kurmark Landwehr, Elbe Landwehr (Sohr)
II Corps Artillery (Röhl)
  3 horse batteries
  2 12pdr batteries
  5 6pdr batteries

III Corps

Thielemann

8th 36th Infantry, 1st Kurmark Landwehr (Borcke)
27th Infantry, 2nd Kurmark Landwehr (Kämpfen)
3rd 4th Kurmark Landwehr (Luck)
31st Infantry, 5th 6th Kurmark Landwehr (Stülpnagel)
III Corps Cavalry (Hobe)
  7th 8th Uhlans, 9th Hussars (Marwitz)
  5th Uhlans, 7th Dragoons,3rd 6th Kurmark Cavalry (Lottum)
III Corps Artillery (Mohnhaupt)
  3 horse batteries
  1 12pdr battery
  2 6pdr batteries

IV Corps

Bülow

10th Infantry, 2nd 3rd Neumark Landwehr (Hacke)
11th Infantry, 1st 2nd Pomeranian Landwehr (Ryssel)
18th Infantry, 3rd 4th Silesian Landwehr (Losthin)
15th Infantry, 1st 2nd Silesian Landwehr (Hiller)
IV Corps Cavalry (Prince William of Prussia)
  1st Uhlans, 2nd 8th Hussars (Sydow)
  10th Hussars, 1st 2nd Neumark Landwehr Cavalry,
  1st 2nd Pomeranian Landwehr Cavalry (Schwerin)
  1st 2nd 3rd Silesian Landwehr Cavalry (Watzdorf)
IV Corps Artillery (Bardeleben)
  3 horse batteries
  3 12pdr batteries
  5 6pdr batteries

▼Prussian Line Infantry: 1, Musketeer, 8th Infantry Regiment (Life Regiment); 2 & 3, Grenadiers, 1st Foot Guards Regiment. The Leib-Regiment was part of von Borcke's brigade of Thielemann's III Corps and fought at Ligny and Wavre. (Bryan Fosten)

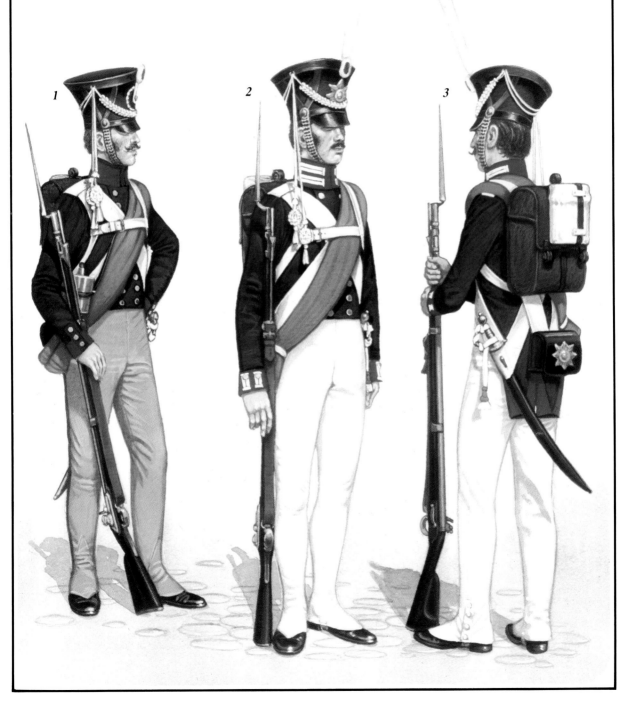

regiments had more troopers than horses. Morale on the whole remained high however. Overall, the cavalry arm was dependable – which is more than could be said of some of Wellington's cavalry, in spite of its being well equipped.

The artillery arm was essentially a good one but had been increased in size by 50 per cent following a decree of April 1815. These new, hastily raised and equipped artillery batteries looked good on paper, but were manned by half-

▲ Private of Prussian Landwehr wearing their typical Litewka coat, cap with oilskin cover and rolled blanket worn bandolier-fashion. (Print by Jacquemain)

trained personnel who had been gleaned from all manner of sources including infantry reserves and depot battalions. They performed well on the field under the circumstances, but the newer batteries were not to be compared with the quality of gunners in French or British/KGL service; their lack of training and experience was manifested by their late arrival in the battles of this campaign.

The Prussians were spread over a very wide area in four corps occupying the area between Wavre, Charleroi, Dinant and Liège/Maastricht. Lines of communication passed through Liège and back to the Rhine – in almost exactly the opposite direction to those of Wellington. Thus, if Napoleon could force either or both armies back along their lines of communication, he would split them apart, and could take on and probably defeat either of the two in detail. With the added benefits of surprise, he might catch at least one of the armies concentrating – and then Brussels would be open.

Wellington had 107,000 men and 216 guns available to him; Blücher had 128,000 infantry and 312 guns. Both forces were very mixed in quality. This compared with the 128,000 men and 366 guns of Napoleon, all volunteers and mostly experienced. If the Allies could operate together in a major action, Napoleon would be outnumbered and outgunned; but in the case of independent action, the odds were almost certainly in favour of the French, whose force had a strong superiority in heavy battle cavalry and a huge and devoted Imperial Guard.

The Prussian and Anglo-Allied armies, being dispersed in a wide arc around and to the south of Brussels in order to ease the strain of forage and supply, would have to be concentrated before they could be used in the field. Their strength as a united force was thus initially well diluted If Napoleon could strike quickly, and with surprise, the chances of catching them individually and in isolation were very good. Given the very wide Prussian dispositions, in the face of a French advance, Napoleon expected Blücher to fall immediately back on his lines of communication and to concentrate towards his headquarters at Namur – in which case it would be left to Wellington to meet the full force of the *Armée du Nord*, even as he was himself concentrating before Brussels.

THE CAMPAIGN OPENS

15-16 June

Although Napoleon immediately made contact with the Prussian outposts of Ziethen's I Corps, he had the full advantage of almost total surprise, and both Wellington's army and the four corps of the Prussian army were still spread over a wide area. Although he probably had not finally decided by this stage which of the two enemy armies he would attack first, Napoleon's plan was to defeat the two armies separately and in detail using the strategy of the central position, forcing himself between the two armies to prevent them uniting and providing local superiority at a chosen battlefield. A swift defeat would force the enemy army back along its supply route, and away from the centre where it could otherwise possibly reinforce the second allied army to the French disadvantage.

To that end the French advanced to, and across, the Sambre in a close formation of corps that arced along the line of the river, the left wing under Ney consisting of I and II Corps with some cavalry detachments from the Guard; the right wing under Grouchy consisting of III Corps and the Cavalry Corps. The remaining two corps, VI Corps and the Guard, were apparently under the direct control of the Emperor himself and brought up the centre rear, to be deployed right or left as the situation demanded.

As the right wing pressed back the outposts of Ziethen's Corps, the Prussians fell back smoothly to the Sambre then northwards, roughly following the main road in the direction of Ligny and Sombreffe. Meanwhile the French left wing moved up the main Charleroi-Brussels road to take the critical crossroads at Quatre Bras. The Guard under Napoleon moved between the two just north of Charleroi, and Lobau's corps was left south of Charleroi on the other side of the Sambre.

Napoleon had further encouraged the Allies to split their forces by pushing two feint attacks wide to the left and right, aiming for Mons and Namur. It nearly worked, for Wellington initially ordered concentration of his army in the direction of Enghien-Braine-Mons – directly away from the Prussians. It was subsequently modified in the early hours of the 16th, with Nivelles selected as the point of concentration, which still gave Napoleon his gap to exploit next day. Blücher, however, showing a distinct hussar mentality, ignored the threat to Namur, where he already had a corps anyway, and actually ordered a forward concentration of his forces behind I Corps.

A forward concentration was really very dangerous. Not only would it deprive Blücher of his IV Corps at Liège in the event of an immediate general action, but it exposed him to critical flanking manoeuvres if anything should go wrong at Namur or if Wellington failed to hold on to his positions on the Prussian right – and, based on his early information, Wellington was concentrating far to the west, leaving Blücher's flanks high 'in the air'. Blücher was unaware of his peril. All it needed was for Ney to follow his orders and advance to the crossroads that night; then at daylight he could immediately fall on the Prussian exposed right flank to achieve the assured destruction of three-quarters of the Prussian army.

So how successful had been Ney's operations that day? In the afternoon Ney had pushed up the main Brussels road but had stopped north of Gosselies to await the arrival of d'Erlon's 20,000 men. He pushed forward the 2,000 cavalry of Lefebvre-Desnouëtes, and these received artillery fire at Frasnes from enemy who immediately retired through the town towards Quatre Bras. Following up to Quatre Bras itself, the cavalry came under significant fire from both artillery and small arms, and halted. The size of the defending force was unclear because of the high corn in the area, and after a few minor probes, by 8 p.m. Ney had ordered camp to be made for the night between Gosselies and Frasnes, then trotted off to meet Napoleon at Charleroi.

Ney had in fact come up against a brigade of Perponcher's Nassauers, who had actually been ordered to move west from Quatre Bras to Nivelles. Without authorization, and in the light of the situation developing to their front, Saxe-

The Campaign Opens, Nights of 14/15 and 15/16 June 181

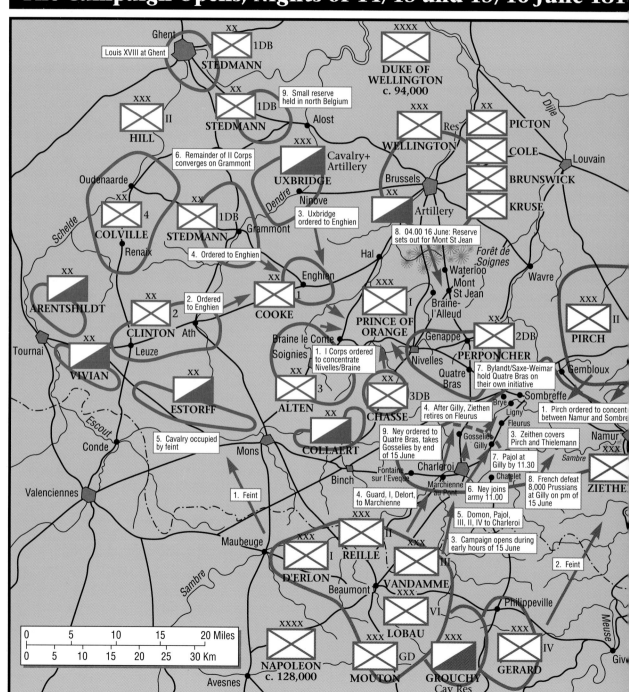

Louis XVIII at Ghent

9. Small reserve held in north Belgium

6. Remainder of II Corps converges on Grammont

3. Uxbridge ordered to Enghien

8. 04.00 16 June: Reserve sets out for Mont St Jean

4. Ordered to Enghien

2. Ordered to Enghien

1. I Corps ordered to concentrate Nivelles/Braine

7. Bylandt/Saxe-Weimar hold Quatre Bras on their own initiative

1. Pirch ordered to concent between Namur and Sombre

4. After Gilly, Ziethen retires on Fleurus

3. Zeithen covers Pirch and Thielemann

5. Cavalry occupied by feint

9. Ney ordered to Quatre Bras, takes Gosselies by end of 15 June

7. Pajol at Gilly by 11.30

8. French defeat 8,000 Prussians at Gilly on pm of 15 June

1. Feint

4. Guard, I, Delort, to Marchienne

6. Ney joins army 11.00

5. Domon, Pajol, III, II, IV to Charleroi

3. Campaign opens during early hours of 15 June

2. Feint

| 0 | 5 | 10 | 15 | 20 Miles |
| 0 | 5 | 10 | 15 | 20 | 25 | 30 Km |

Weimar and Perponcher had chosen to stay. By stalling the French south of Quatre Bras, these very able officers had saved valuable time for the Allies to recover, for it was only very late at the Duchess of Richmond's ball held that night in

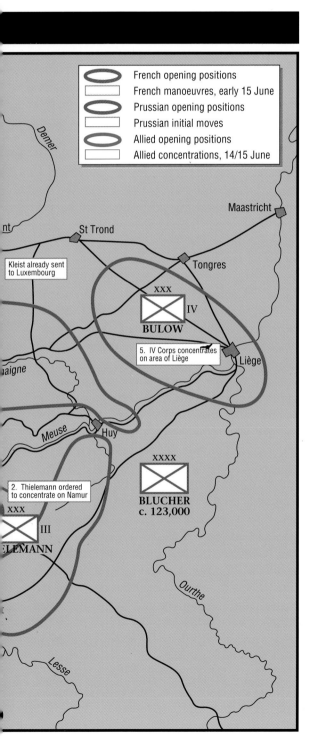

French opening positions
French manoeuvres, early 15 June
Prussian opening positions
Prussian initial moves
Allied opening positions
Allied concentrations, 14/15 June

Maastricht

St Trond

Kleist already sent
to Luxembourg

Tongres

XXX
IV
BULOW

5. IV Corps concentrates
on area of Liège

Liège

Meuse   Huy

Demer

nt

aigne

XXXX
BLUCHER
c. 123,000

2. Thielemann ordered
to concentrate on Namur

XXX

III
ELEMANN

Ourthe

Lesse

Brussels that events became clearer to Wellington. During the course of the ball came news confirming the French move towards Mons as a feint, together with first reports of action at Quatre Bras. Wellington had indeed been 'humbugged' into deploying his army too far west, perhaps as a result of his sensitivity concerning his lines of communication. Realizing the full extent of developments, he countermanded his previous orders and shifted the weight of his army to his inner flank, towards Nivelles-Quatre Bras, and it was not until 4 a.m. on the 16th that Picton's Reserve Division started on the road south to Mont St. Jean to the tune of 'Highland Laddie', followed at 8 a.m. by Wellington and his staff.

Meanwhile in the French headquarters at Charleroi, Napoleon was still unaware of the forward concentration of Blücher's army. He was expecting Wellington to fall back towards Brussels, putting both time and space between himself and Napoleon as he concentrated his forces and only then turning to fight. However, with the French well-justified reputation for rapid manoeuvre, Napoleon would surely attack him before he could gather his army together. Thus, as Ney left Napoleon at Charleroi, his verbal orders stated that the main thrust on the 16th would be against the British, and Ney would be expecting the French Reserve to support his two corps next day. Events would soon overtake them. For the moment, Perponcher at Quatre Bras, now reinforced by Bylandt, had just 8,000 men, 16 guns and 50 hussars to face Ney's initial 25,000 infantry, 3,000 cavalry and 60 guns, with a further 20,000 men of d'Erlon's corps coming up from just to their south, and VI Corps and the Guard also expected. The odds for the Dutch-Belgians were long indeed.

16-17 June

It was Napoleon's usual habit to dictate his orders at about 2 a.m. so that they could reach the army before 6 a.m. for early operations. On the 16th, however, exhausted after the exertions of the previous days, he did not confirm his verbal orders to Ney in writing until 6 a.m., and this message did not leave the inexperienced HQ staff until some two hours later.

Fortunately for Wellington, the forward concentration of Blücher's army became known to Napoleon at mid-morning of the 16th, and what was originally to be a pinning action by Grouchy at Ligny was turned into plans for a general engagement. Unfortunately for Ney, in all the excitement, no-one wrote to him until after 2 p.m. to tell him that the weight of the French army was now to be directed against the Prussians that day. By the time he received the dispatch, it had turned 4 p.m.

Expecting Wellington to withdraw to gather his army, the majority of Ney's force had bivouacked in line of march along the road, ready for pursuit and manoeuvre rather than in line of battle. Amazingly, Ney issued no preparatory orders to his troops as he returned from his meeting with Napoleon, and, as most of his force was spread out over fifteen miles, it would be impossible to make immediate headway the next morning. Furthermore, Ney waited for the written confirmation of his orders to arrive from Charleroi before he started the morning's operations. As these only left headquarters at 8 a.m., Ney did not receive them until after 10.30. These clearly told him to 'hold yourself in readiness for an immediate advance towards Brussels once the Reserve reaches you'. Without any sense of urgency, at 11.00 Ney issued his orders to Reille to concentrate on Quatre Bras.

Meanwhile, Wellington had arrived at Quatre Bras to see the position for himself. Finding it quiet, and seeing the French preparing a meal, he rode over to meet Blücher at Ligny and promised to come to his help if he were not attacked himself. It was probably at this point that he finally decided to concentrate in strength on Quatre Bras rather than Nivelles, and to that end he called up Picton's Division – which had been waiting at the Mont St. Jean crossroads in readiness to move to either location – to join Perponcher's troops.

Before Quatre Bras, Ney totally wasted the morning, and it was not until 2 p.m. that Reille started his attack.

The Battle of Quatre Bras, 16 June

Reille had seen the British in the Peninsula and had seen many a reputation lost there by French overconfidence and rash attacks. He knew of Wellington's methods of hiding large parts of his army until the last minute; so, noting that the undulating terrain provided plenty of scope for concealment in the tall rye, and that Bossu Wood was a perfect position for a flank ambush, he advanced with extreme caution.

Perponcher, now under the newly arrived Prince of Orange, had covered his entire front with the 27th Jägers in a thin line that stretched for almost a mile. Behind and to the west of the road stood his remaining battalions – some lining the Bossu Wood – and with the 5th Militia occupying the Gemioncourt farm.

To the east of the road, the French 5th Division under Bachelu advanced behind a strong skirmish line and soon pressed against Gemioncourt as the opposing skirmishers fell back to the farm, but they found this initially a stubborn defence. Jérôme's 6th Division, arriving late, advanced to the west of the road also behind a skirmishing line and pressed up towards Bossu Wood. Within an hour, with the support of artillery, the outposts of Pireaumont and Gemioncourt had finally been taken, and Jérôme was moving steadily through Bossu Wood as the weight of numbers told on Bylandt's thin line, which was retiring in good order and in expectation of reinforcements from Picton. Suddenly a cavalry charge was hurled against the 17th Dutch Light Infantry, which fragmented before it, some rushing headlong to the rear, others remaining in isolated groups of men fighting to the last before being ridden down. The terribly thin line had been breached, Piré's lancers breaking through the centre in a spirited charge that routed Merlen's lighter Dutch cavalry as they tried to stem the tide. Had Reille started just a short while earlier, with nothing to stop the exploitation of the break in the Allied line, the battle would have now been over almost before it had started; but in the very nick of time, Picton's division – including many veteran units – arrived at Quatre Bras with Wellington to check the French advance.

Perhaps remembering Reille's advice about Wellington's wily tactics in sheltering his troops from sight until the last moment, the advancing French infantry stopped when they unexpectedly met fresh troops, then withdrew; but the lancers came on, some breaking off to surround pockets of Dutch troops, others heading straight for the Highlanders who, forming square, issued a volley that repulsed the remains of the attack.

Under Wellington's personal supervision, the British brigades now lined the hedged Namur road to the east of the crossroads, the 95th Rifles occupying the wood just to the north of Lac Materne, where they engaged and just held Bachelu's advancing tirailleurs, the 92nd occupying the buildings at the crossroads itself. The Hanoverians were placed behind them and to the north of the Namur road, and the arrival of Brunswick to the west of Quatre Bras completed the line in time to meet the next French attack. Bylandt's line was by now almost totally in ruins having been heavily outnumbered from the start and having faced a well organized combined-arms attack. Many of his troops had headed for the comparative safety of Bossu Wood.

Ney's artillery now turned its full force on to Picton's units, who were ordered by Wellington to lie down in the shelter of the ditches and the partly sunken road. This sunken road and its thick hedges provided valuable cover to Picton's men, as they sheltered from the 38-gun French bombardment that now opened up in anticipation of the renewed assault, the French columns being organized by Ney in person. He formed four columns, each of brigade strength and with a mass that he was convinced would smash straight through the thin lines to bring immediate victory.

As the four French columns of infantry advanced, screening their cannon, the bombardment subsided, and Wellington ordered Picton's troops over the hedges, to stand silently beside the Brunswick infantry to their right, near the wood. In Picton's ranks, the long, thin, silent lines were waiting calmly as the French came on with cries of 'On to victory!', 'Give them the bayonet!' and 'Vive l'Empereur!' Even for Napoleon's veterans of 1813/14, the sight of a British line must have been a perplexing novelty, and one can perhaps visualize during this attack how an initial French confidence could have turned to panic during the few minutes it took for the French columns to assault the steady British lines.

▲ *Friedrich Wilhelm, Duke of Brunswick (1771-1815), commander of the Brunswick forces in the Waterloo campaign, and killed at Quatre Bras. This depicts the Duke in the black uniform with* *death's-head badge of his Brunswick contingent.* (Print from Ackermann's Repository of Arts)

At the start, the general bulk and massing together of large numbers gave the columns an initial sense of security, stemming from safety in numbers. The spectacle and confidence of the French column, advancing to shouts and cheers, loud inspiring music and much waving of banners, bristling muskets and even shakos held aloft had always intimidated their continental opponents when they had met it deployed in line, and the continental armies had learned early on that their troops in the open would almost always break before contact if they did not use a deeper, column formation themselves. But today this must have been a very new experience for many of the French, as Picton's steady infantry waited silently to receive them – why were the British standing? Could they not see that the French would be through them in moments? Why did they not move? The columns moved quickly through the now-flattened corn, through long musket range

The Battle of Quatre Bras, 16 June 1815

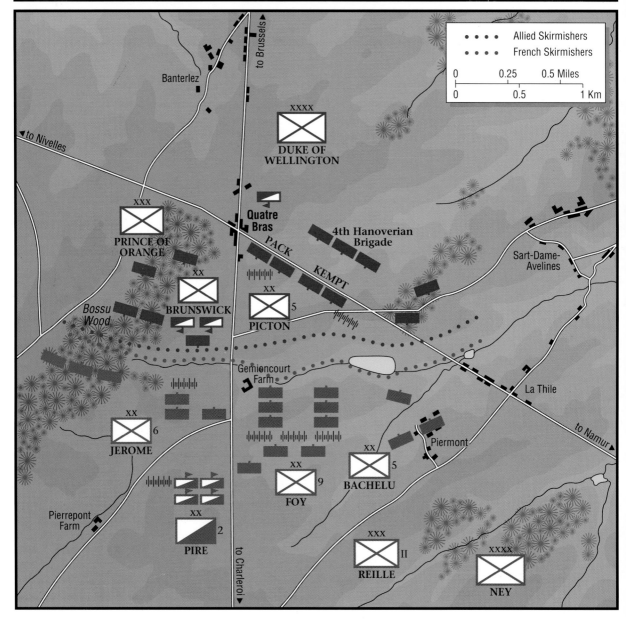

and into close range. Why did the British still not open fire? The impact of a volley at this range would be horrific.

The clear, English voice rose from the line of red ahead: 'Present!' As one, the muskets rose silently to the firing position, pointing directly at the heads of the columns from far to their left and right, an overlapping fire they knew would be deadly. It was too late to turn back now.

'Fire!' All along the line the British volleys smashed into the heads of the advancing columns, proving once again the mathematical certainty of the superiority of a steady British line over a French column. To the east of the main Brussels road, the heads of the splendid blue columns of infantry that just a few minutes before seemed ready to crash through the thin lines before them had become a reeling, confused mass of dying and wounded men. Screams of agony burst from the collapsed and maimed, the once reassuring mass of the column now working against it as following ranks of their comrades stumbled over the mangled remains at their feet and, moving onwards, themselves became victims of the rolling, precision fire of Wellington's veterans. The front now halted in total confusion, trying to deploy to return fire, the rear of the column still pressing them forward

▲ *'Quatre Bras': British infantry in square as portrayed by Lady Elizabeth Butler. One of the highlights of the 1875 Royal Academy* *exhibition, it was described by Ruskin as the first Pre-Raphaelite battle painting.*

over the bloody mess beneath their feet. With confusion and disorder in the columns at its height, through the smoke came the shrieking war cries heralding the wild, downhill charge of Picton's Highlanders. The shattered columns fled to escape their retribution.

Against the youthful and less experienced Brunswickers to the west of the road, however, Jérôme was having significantly more success, and the Brunswick line broke as most of the remaining Belgians flocked to the rear. Jérôme's men swept unstoppably through Bossu Wood. French cavalry were coming up to exploit the opening, and the Duke of Brunswick launched a rash counter-attack with his 'Death's Head' Hussars, which was decimated by French musketry on the way in, and routed on contact by Piré's cavalry. The Duke of Brunswick himself fell a casualty, as the French cavalry chased the now broken Hussars. The counter-attack had cost heavy losses, including six cannon; but it had stopped what might have

developed into a rout and given the infantry some respite in which to fall back and try to regroup beyond the wood.

Successful on his left but checked on his right, Ney called up d'Erlon to help his drive for the vital crossroads. But to his consternation he found no sign of I Corps behind him. It was by then around 4 p.m., still with a numerical advantage, when Ney received an order from Napoleon (timed 2 p.m.), instructing him to take the crossroads and then fall on the Prussian right and rear. With Reille's corps already fully committed, Ney bade d'Erlon hasten to deliver what he thought was the *coup de grâce*, for already his cavalry were roaming freely through Wellington's right and centre.

Piré had hurled his chasseurs and lancers once more at the Allied centre in a surprise attack that took them almost to the crossroads itself, Wellington himself having had to leap the (prone) ranks of the 92nd to evade the French charge. The cavalry was by now somewhat disordered, as it circled round behind the hastily formed square of the 92nd, before swinging south to take the adjacent 42nd and 44th – still formed in line – in

▲Quatre Bras: the 28th (North Gloucestershire) Regiment repel a French attack; the mounted officer in left background is the unit's commander, Sir Charles Belson. (Print by S. Mitan after Captain George Jones)

the rear. The undulating terrain and remaining corn concealed the charge until the last minute and took the British troops almost completely by surprise. The 42nd Highlanders, caught in the rear in the act of forming square, incredibly managed to complete the square with some of the lancers trapped inside. After a vicious mêlée that cost the 42nd dear, especially among their officers, the Highlanders killed nearly every one of the now trapped lancers, before throwing their bodies out of the square. Next to them the 44th were caught by the same charge – too late even to begin to form square. But with total coolness the rear rank was ordered to about face and gave forth a series of volleys that were sufficient to repel the half-pressed charge of both the lancers and the chasseurs that followed them.

The French cavalry, by now totally disordered, retired to the French lines, and the respite allowed

Wellington to redeploy some of his troops to stop the rot on his right flank. The attack now settled down to a close-range slogging match, where the superior firepower of the British troops to the centre and east of the battlefield slowly began to take its toll – despite being partly still in square against the possibility of enemy cavalry in the area. Two more cavalry charges to the east of the Brussels road routed a Hanoverian battalion but otherwise made no impact on Wellington's steady squares.

The initiative was slipping from Ney's grasp. Its delicate balance was now tilting towards the Allies. They had held against the best that Ney could throw against them, and fresh reinforcements in the form of Halkett's and Kielmansegge's brigades from Alten's division were arriving to bolster Wellington's strength. The French right was actually starting to fall back. Ney's tired army was losing its superiority of numbers over troops who had already proven themselves well prepared for a fight and who were commanded by one of the world's great generals. Worse still for Ney, it was at this point that he learned of the true whereabouts of d'Erlon.

Some time earlier, d'Erlon's corps been ordered to Ligny by an aide, General de la Bedoyère. Far from his arrival being imminent at Quatre Bras, d'Erlon was actually already well on his way to Ligny, every minute taking him farther from the crisis now looming for Ney. To save time, de la Bedoyere had not consulted Ney before ordering the corps to Ligny in the name of the Emperor. One can only imagine the spirit in which the fiery, red-headed Ney received this news at so critical a juncture in the battle – that he was the last to be told was simply to add insult to injury.

Meanwhile, Wellington was not a commander to sit idly by in such circumstances. A sweeping counter-attack by Alten's troops on the recoiling French right made the situation critical for the French, and the impetuous Ney immediately decided that he should recall d'Erlon. Not pausing to consider how long it would take for the order to reach him, nor how long it would be before that corps would appear at Quatre Bras, Ney's almost reflex reaction effectively took this force out of both the Ligny and Quatre Bras engagements.

Then at 5 p.m., finally outnumbered by Wellington, under pressure on his right, with that flank actually retiring, with no reserves, and incensed and frustrated almost beyond control at the day's muddles and lack of success against his very able opponents, he received a 'hurry up' message from the Emperor. It was the last straw. Not only had the previously promised Emperor's troops never arrived, he had actually been robbed of troops critical to the success of his operations. Napoleon clearly had no appreciation of the fact that Ney was hard pressed and now facing most of Wellington's army. With no reserves, he needed time to stabilize his line and reform his right. There was only one thing left to throw at the Allies, and in a fit of desperation Ney ordered the recently arrived cavalry of Kellermann to make an almost suicidal charge into the Allied lines – a brigade of cavalry against an entire army. It would be to throw away an irreplaceable force in exchange for just a few minutes of respite. Such is the logic of war and the value of life to some military minds. Kellermann rightly questioned the order, for only part of his brigade had reached the field, namely Guiton's brigade of 750 men of the 8th and 11th Cuirassier Regiments (the latter not even having cuirasses). Ney would have none of it. Promising him support from the depleted ranks of Piré's cavalry, Ney dismissed him abruptly with, 'Go! But go now!'

Kellermann's regiments moved up beneath the crest of Gemioncourt ridge, out of sight of the British infantry beyond. The 42nd Highlanders and the 2/44th were still in square to the east of the Charleroi road, having already been mauled by Piré's lancers. The 92nd Highlanders were in a square that actually straddled the Charleroi road, and Wellington himself was still sheltering there.

The cavalry deployed silently into line below the crest. The clear notes of the trumpet finally signalled the charge, and Kellermann unleashed the brigade forward, straight into charge speed – dispensing with the customary build up via walk/trot/canter. The brigade thundered towards the British squares, scattering the remnants of the Brunswick and Belgian cavalry in their path. The battered squares held firm, offering a deadly fire that broke up the charge and caused the horsemen

▼*King's German Legion: 1, Sergeant, Sharpshooters, 2nd Light Battalion; 2, Officer, 2nd Light Battalion; 3, Private, 1st Light Battalion. Two companies of the 1st and six of the 2nd were almost wiped out in the defence of La Haye Sainte farm. (Bryan Fosten)*

to flow around the leading squares, disordered but not halted, now thundering on towards Halkett's Brigade.

A few minutes previously, as Kellermann's units were preparing to charge, Colin Halkett – in Alten's 3rd Division, in the Prince of Orange's I Corps – was leading his fresh brigade up. In Picton's adjacent division, Pack's brigade had been under serious pressure for some two hours; casualties were mounting and ammunition was running low. With the arrival of the fresh troops, the second battalion of the 69th (South Lincolnshire) Regiment was ordered to Pack to bolster his position. Halkett therefore moved up, handed the unit over to him and went back to bring up the remainder of his brigade. Pack ordered the 69th to form square before moving farther along his brigade.

The Prince of Orange, however, not understanding what was happening, found the 69th in the act of forming square. Being perhaps somewhat piqued that an officer from another corps was messing about with 'his' battalion, he ordered them back into line again. There were protests. The Prince insisted. And it was while the infantry were in the middle of this manoeuvre that Kellerman's cuirassiers, now emerging past the leading British squares, fell upon them from the flank. For the 2/69th, it was too late to reform into square. Two companies only were able to turn to face the onslaught before they were isolated from the main body and hacked down to a man. It was a desperate situation for the 69th. Garavaque's troops thrust into the very heart of the unformed battalion, aiming for the colours (the capture of which qualified for a bounty). In the Colour Party, Ensign Duncan Keith was immediately and ruthlessly slain by cuirassier Lami; the King's Colour he held was prised from his dying grip and carried triumphantly to the rear. Volunteer Christopher Clark, carrying the Regimental flag, killed three cuirassiers in its defence. He was only marginally luckier, however, for although he was able to get his Regimental Colour to safety, he incurred no less than 22 wounds in the process.

With nothing capable of stopping the charge, the 69th made for the shelter of Bossu Wood. Unchecked, Kellermann drove forward, ruthlessly hacked down the crew of an artillery battery and headed on towards the nearby 33rd, who were also unformed. Shaken by the fate of their comrades of the 69th, they too fled towards the wood, where they could reform in safety. Next in the line of charge, the 2/30th had just been able to form square in time and had easily repulsed the 11th Cuirassiers, while a nearby square of the now unsteady Brunswickers dissolved in the presence of the French cavalry.

Wherever friendly troops cleared the British lines, French artillery remorselessly pounded the dense targets of the British infantry squares, and Ney had thrown in all the infantry support he could scrape together. But it was not enough. The supporting attacks were slowly grinding to a halt. Elements of Piré's tired and reformed division had by now also come up, as Kellerman pushed forward almost to the crossroads itself. There, blown from the charge, deep in Wellington's lines, disordered by the mêlées and with no local infantry support, the cavalry came under a murderous cross-fire from the 30th, 73rd and a battery of the KGL as Kellermann tried to reorganize his command.

The French infantry supporting attacks were now being firmly repulsed, and every British regiment was being alerted to bring down the heavy cavalrymen who had done so much damage but who were now in considerable disorder. Parties of Highlanders were able to range the field relatively safely in active pursuit of Kellerman's cuirassiers, exacting a bloody revenge for the terrible toll of the afternoon; while scattered parties of French cavalry remnants were also roaming about. There were plenty of lucky escapes for troops on both sides. In one section of the field, for example, one of a troop of cuirassiers killing wounded Scots came upon a major of the 42nd who had been badly hurt. As the cuirassier stabbed at the major, the major grasped him and pulled him off his horse and on to the ground, where they grappled in hand to hand combat. A French lancer came to the cuirassier's aid, and thrust at the major as he struggled with his foe. Rolling away from the lance thrust, the major managed to pull the cuirassier over him, interposing him to take the full brunt of the lance thrust as Highlanders rushing to his aid dispatched the mounted lancer in his turn.

Meanwhile at the crossroads the remains of Kellermann's blown charge was being shot to pieces. In a hail of fire from Wellington's battered ranks, the decimated cavalry fled in disorder to the safety of the French lines. Kellermann himself had his horse shot from beneath him and only managed to return safely from the charge by clinging to the stirrups of two of his men. For no significant gain, the charge had cost him more than a third of his magnificent brigade. Even as the cavalry retired to the safety of the French lines, Wellington was being further reinforced by the 5,000 crack troops of the British Guards Division, who stormed into Bossu Wood.

Ney's was a spent force. There was no longer any question of his taking Quatre Bras, only the possibility of holding Wellington at bay. There was nothing he could do when, at around 6.30, in typical form, Wellington realized that the French had shot their bolt and ordered a large-scale counter-attack across his entire front. By 7.30 p.m. Bossu Wood was back in Allied hands, the Allies had taken Pireaumont, and advanced to Gemioncourt brook. By 9 p.m., in the rapidly fading light, the battle was over. Ney had been pushed back to his starting positions, and the battle had ended in a tactical draw. As dusk turned to night, Wellington's British cavalry and Royal Horse Artillery reinforced his position – just too late to participate in the battle.

Strategically, Wellington had at last managed to get his army together. He now had confidence in many of his previously unproven troops, who in their turn must have established something of a moral ascendancy over their opponents of the day. Further, his lines of communications were untouched, and he had control of a road network that could take him in any direction he wanted: forward to link with the Prussians (if they had won at Ligny), north to cover Brussels, or back towards the Channel ports. For the first time in the campaign, Wellington was properly ready to control his destiny.

Losses in the battle were about 4,300 for the French, while Wellington had lost 2,275 British, 369 Hanoverians, and 819 Brunswickers, but substantial numbers of the wounded on both sides appear to have been able to return to the ranks within 24 hours or so. No separate return could be made for the Dutch-Belgian troops, a great many of whom had left the field by the end of the day, or had headed for the relative security of Bossu Wood. As the day closed, and having fought the French to a standstill, Wellington's next move would depend on the Prussians at Ligny.

The Battle of Ligny, 16 June

The unexpected forward deployment of Blücher's army lining up on the morning of the 16th awaiting his assault made this very much an opportunist battle for Napoleon. The Prussians had based their defence along the Ligny, a small but marshy stream that was difficult to cross except at its four bridges. Ten villages and hamlets had been prepared and incorporated into the defence line, which helped to cover all four of the bridging points and thereby deny them to Napoleon. Rising ground to the rear made an advantageous position for the supporting Prussian columns.

There were flaws in the position, however. By following the Ligny stream, Blücher's line formed a salient that was open to flanking artillery fire; by the same token, troops placed on the forward slopes of the hills would be exposed to massed artillery fire without being able to advance across the Ligny to engage.

Napoleon's plan was simple. He would use his cavalry to keep the Prussian left flank busy, while with his superior numbers he engaged in a frontal assault on the Prussian centre and right. After a massive artillery bombardment and attrition by his infantry, part of Ney's forces would be ready to appear on the Prussian right wing. As this force enveloped their right, Napoleon would smash through their centre with his Guard, to destroy almost all of the Prussian army at a stroke. There had been no sound of gunfire from Quatre Bras during the morning, so Napoleon assumed Ney had occupied the crossroads without a hitch, and was probably already on his way to Ligny: 'In three hours' time the campaign will be decided. If Ney carries out his orders thoroughly not a gun of the Prussian army will get away.'

▲ *Napoleon and his staff survey the field of Ligny, 16 June 1815. (Painting by G. Weiss)*

At approximately 2.30 p.m. the battle started. In the excitement and heat of combat, however, the 10,000 men of Lobau's VI Corps at Charleroi had been completely forgotten, and Napoleon's staff had also forgotten to inform Marshal Ney that his presence would be required at Ligny at his earliest convenience. Later in the day, Napoleon was to wish dearly that he had access to even one of these two forces.

The fighting was hard from the very start, and by engaging across Blücher's whole front Napoleon stopped him being able to redeploy troops in his forward line. Even in the early stages of the battle, although Blücher had numerical superiority, he had to make good losses from his reserves. These in their turn were subjected to a heavy bombardment as they waited on the forward slopes of the hills.

The western end of the battlefield was particularly important to each side, enabling as it did communication and possible reinforcement for both parties with their friendly troops – Ney for the French, and Wellington for the Prussians. The fighting here was particularly vicious, and with no quarter given or asked for, Prussians and Frenchmen tore at each other in hand-to-hand combat, every shattered, burning building in the villages contested right to the very end. Prisoners taken were ruthlessly slain. Around the villages of Ligny and St. Amand losses were very heavy on both sides. The fighting for Ligny village was particularly bloody, but after five attempts involving very intense hand to hand action, the surviving French forces finally succeeded in prising part of it from the Prussian grip. Losses of up to 60 per cent were reported by the French units at Ligny itself.

By 3.15 p.m., shattered by artillery fire from the flanks, and seeing the French pouring into

The Battle of Ligny, 16 June 1815

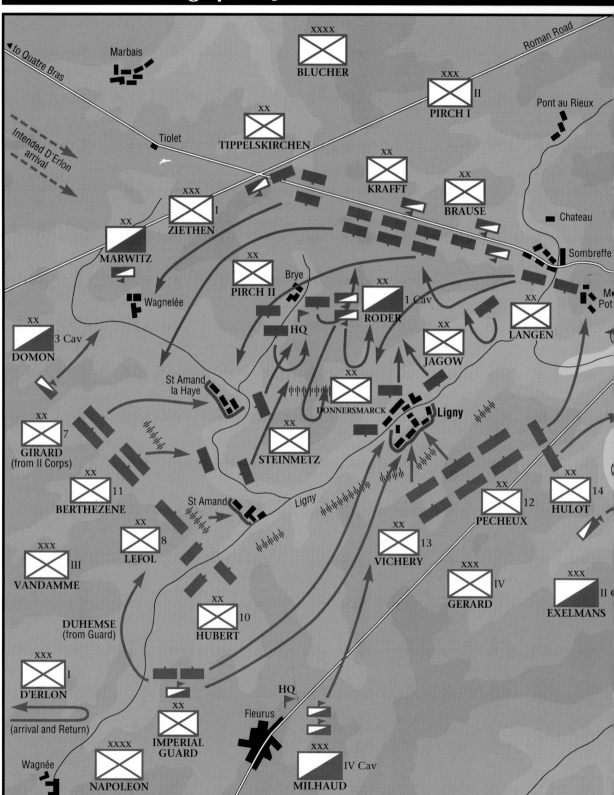

to Quatre Bras

Marbais

Roman Road

XXXX
BLUCHER

XXX
II
PIRCH I

Pont au Rieux

Intended D'Erlon
arrival

Tiolet

XX
TIPPELSKIRCHEN

XX
KRAFFT

XX
BRAUSE

Chateau

XXX
I
ZIETHEN

XX
MARWITZ

Brye

XX
PIRCH II

XX
RODER
1 Cav

Sombreffe

M
Pot

XX
LANGEN

Wagnelée

XX
3 Cav
DOMON

HQ

XX
JAGOW

XX
GIRARD
(from II Corps)
7

St Amand
la Haye

XX
DONNERSMARCK

Ligny

XX
11
BERTHEZENE

XX
STEINMETZ

St Amand

Ligny

XX
12
PECHEUX

XX
14
HULOT

XX
8
LEFOL

XXX
III
VANDAMME

XX
13
VICHERY

XXX
IV
GERARD

XXX
II C
EXELMANS

DUHEMSE
(from Guard)

XX
10
HUBERT

XXX
I
D'ERLON

HQ

Fleurus

(arrival and Return)

XX
IMPERIAL
GUARD

Wagnée

XXXX
NAPOLEON

XXX
IV Cav
MILHAUD

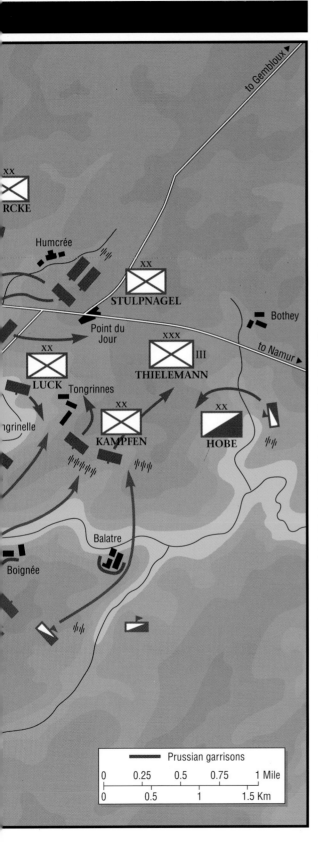

Ligny, the Prussian salient began collapsing. The majority of Blücher's force was now committed to prop up his line and fill the huge gaps scythed by the artillery bombardment. Now was the time for Napoleon to send in his Guard in conjunction with d'Erlon's flanking manoeuvre. But where was d'Erlon? As he ordered the Guard forward to form up, Napoleon sent an urgent appeal to Ney to hasten to his aid: 'The fate of France is in your hands . . . do not hesitate even for a moment to . . . direct your advance on the heights of St. Amand.' Ney had received this message at 5 p.m.

Unable to wait any longer for Ney or d'Erlon, Napoleon formed up his Guard to smash through the crumbling Prussian centre. But at 5.30, just as the assault was about to roll forward, an alarm spread along the lines. A long column of troops was appearing behind the French left flank. Scouts reported it as hostile. Had Wellington broken through? It could not be d'Erlon – it was in the wrong place. Clearly Napoleon could not risk committing the Guard at such a time, and the attack was postponed while aides galloped to the column to determine its status.

It was, in fact, d'Erlon. A poorly written order had ordered him to conduct his march on 'Wagnée' instead of 'Wagnelé'; hence his arrival at completely the wrong place. In addition, he had failed to push out advance orderlies to warn friendly troops of his arrival. So the resultant surprise had not only delayed a critical attack but had caused the French left (under Vandamme) to become decidedly nervous, so that the Young Guard had to be deployed to bolster them, and at one stage General Lefol had been forced to turn his own artillery on to his panic-stricken men as they deserted the line.

It was only by about 6.30 that the true situation was made clear, and the Guard could roll forward. In that respite Blücher had consolidated his line and had even pressed the wavering French left with a scratch force to retake part of St. Amand. With almost incredible irony, even as the Guard formation was being re-assembled, the news came that d'Erlon's corps, now clearly in sight of the Prussians, had just turned around to march back to Quatre Bras with almost all of its troops. Ney's order of recall had arrived.

Nevertheless, for the Prussians the final act had begun. The Young Guard threw them out of St. Amand, and by 7.30 the grand assault was ready to be launched into the very heart of the reformed Prussian positions. More than two hundred guns opened up on the desperately thin Prussian centre. Then at 7.45, as a thunder storm broke over the battlefield, more than six thousand men of the Guard marched forward in a combined arms assault that swept back into Ligny and smashed into the Prussian lines. The 21st Prussian Regiment charged the advancing grenadiers, but were intercepted by the accompanying French cuirassiers and thoroughly mauled. Two squadrons of the 1st Westphalian Landwehr cavalry were sacrificed as they charged the disciplined ranks of the Guard to absolutely no avail as the French swept on and through the village. Nothing could save the battle for the Prussians now, but Blücher could still save his army from the worst horrors of pursuit if he could just buy some time.

Blücher positioned himself at the head of Röder's cavalry and hurled it at the advancing French Guard. It was a forlorn hope. The Guard's squares easily beat off the attack, Lützow himself falling wounded at the head of the shattered 6th Uhlans, now down to only 300 men. A further

▲Napoleon gives the order for the final advance to break the Prussian position at Ligny; the ADC wears hussar uniform, and at the right the Imperial Guard infantry awaits the order to advance. (Print after J. Grenier)

▼ Major von Lützow, who raised one of the first Freikorps for the Prussian Army in 1813; in the Waterloo campaign its members served in 25th Infantry, 6th Uhlans and 9th Hussars. (Engraving by Guiseppe Longhi)

charge was launched at the squares by two more regiments of Prussian cavalry, but suddenly from the flank came a charge by the supporting French cuirassiers, which smashed into the reeling Prussian attack. A succession of piecemeal cavalry charges were similarly repulsed as the squares of the Guard cooly met the attacking Prussians with measured volleys before the remnants of the broken cavalry were scooped up by the omnipresent French cuirassiers.

Blücher himself had fallen in one of the charges as his horse was shot. He lay there, pinned for some time as French cuirassiers repeatedly swept by, over terrain packed with bodies where

▼Blücher's accident at Ligny: pinned under his horse, the old marshal was ridden-over and extricated only with difficulty. Until he had recovered, direction of the *action and the withdrawal from Ligny passed to Gneisenau. (Print after R. F. Messerschmitt)*

he and many others had fallen during the day. It was well after dark before a faithful aide finally managed to drag him out and take him to the rear, where liberal applications of gin and garlic revived him enough to rejoin his army.

Meanwhile, the Prussians were in a state of confusion, with no leader and an army retiring in disarray looking to put time and distance between it and the inevitable French pursuit. The general staff had to agree quickly among themselves where to go to regroup, for they had already been pushed back from the main routes to Namur, their principal line of communication. And so, in poor light at the drizzly roadside, Gneisenau and the corps commanders met to decide an alternative route for the battered force. The only name on the maps clearly visible to all was Wavre, somewhat to the north of Ligny. So it was that Wavre was chosen as a first stage before retiring eastward towards Liège. By almost pure accident, it was the one place Napoleon did not expect, and the one

▲ *A fusilier NCO of the 6th Infantry Regiment (1st West Prussian) wearing the new tunic worn by* *some formations during the Hundred Days Campaign. (Bryan Fosten)*

direction that would allow the Prussians the slightest option of joining up with Wellington before Brussels. Not that Gneisenau had any intention of moving to join Wellington; not only was he highly suspicious of his allies, almost to the point of Anglophobia in fact, but he was fully expecting the French pursuit to keep him fully occupied as he fell back.

But – amazingly – as the Prussian army withdrew from the battlefield, the anticipated French pursuit did not materialize. Although deserters fled in droves, the majority of the army was able to keep maintain cohesion and retire unmolested on Wavre. The pursuit was actually late in coming at the direct order and responsibility of the Emperor. After the battle he made Ligny his headquarters and, hoping and believing the Prussians to be totally crushed, he refused to allow a rigorous pursuit that night. Perhaps here again we can see the evidence of the over-optimism and missing energy that only a few years before would have galvanized his cavalry into immediate and aggressive pursuit. After Jena, for example, the French pursuit was so vigorous that it lasted almost to the Baltic, and ended the entire campaign.

17 June: Interlude of Missed Opportunities

Napoleon was not at all well on the night of the 16th. The following day, drained from the effects of the battle and his illness, Napoleon was struck with an overpowering lethargy and depression that lasted the whole morning of the 17th, which he spent touring the grisly battlefield with Grouchy and his staff. He refused repeated requests by Grouchy to start his pursuit, preferring to wait for news from Ney about the battle at Quatre Bras. It was late morning before the arrival of Ney's report on that battle caused him to realize the implications of his position and the opportunity that was offered of outflanking Wellington's force at Quatre Bras. It snapped him into action. Grouchy was belatedly sent after the Prussians, presumed to be retreating towards Namur, and Ney was ordered to pin the Allied line ready for Napoleon to swing in behind its flank and complete the destruction Ney had begun on the previous day.

Preparations were made, aides hurrying far

and wide to spur Ney to action and to release Grouchy's forces. But for the Prussians the respite had already had considerable implications. The main Prussian force had been allowed to disengage from the French army and to retire intact upon Wavre, where it was able in part to regroup around the unmolested IV Corps. Further, because of the delay in the French pursuit, contact with the main body had been broken, and instead of heading north towards the main Prussian force, Grouchy headed north-east towards where he expected the Prussians to be. He was pressing merely against the dregs of the army – the eight thousand stragglers and deserters who had been able to reach the road heading for the safety of Namur.

Ironically, as Grouchy's pursuit innocently headed north-east, he was describing a wide arc that could ultimately help to place the Prussian army between the French and British forces and drive the two Allies together.

Meanwhile, Napoleon was preparing to out-flank the British at Quatre Bras while they were held by Ney's forces resuming the fight of the previous day. But something was very suspiciously wrong on his left wing. Hearing no cannon fire by lunchtime, Napoleon hastened over to Ney's position to find the troops still eating lunch and the attack yet to start. Against a general of the calibre of Wellington, a vital opportunity had almost certainly been thrown away.

And so it transpired. In contrast to Napoleon's inaction, Wellington had lost no time during the night of the 16th in determining the fate of the Prussian army and the direction of its retreat. The realization of his extreme danger caused him to prepare to withdraw. When, inexplicably, no French attack was immediately forthcoming on the 17th, he started thinning his line and sending back the transports and wounded to his position at Mont St. Jean. He would be prepared to fight there if Blücher would commit to send even a single corps to his aid. By the time the French had realized their error, it was already too late, and Wellington's main force had slipped away, leaving an angry Emperor to berate in frustration his wing commander who had shown such inertia.

To cap it all, the weather broke as the French forces came up. Rain churned the roads into thick mud, and the chances of catching up with Welling-ton's army dwindled as the afternoon wore on. Finally, any remaining potential for French pro-gress was easily hindered by Wellington's rear-guard of cavalry and horse artillery as it fought a successful holding action during the evening rains.

His successful withdrawal during the 17th took him to a ridge line south of Mont St. Jean, a position that had been carefully noted by Welling-ton and his staff some time ago as being an excellent defensive location. Even the Forest of Soignes to his rear was an asset, allowing infantry to melt through it if retreat proved necessary but hindering any pursuing cavalry. The outlying farms along the front of the position and the Chateau de Hougoumont provided excellent strongpoints that would be hard to overcome and which could offer flanking fire to any enemy attacking past them – thereby 'funnelling' attacks on to the centre. In fact the original position Wellington had favoured was the ridge around La Belle Alliance, where the French massed battery was later to be positioned, but Delancey had opted for the shorter line north of it during the retreat.

Napoleon's elation that he had finally cornered Wellington was tempered only by his concern that he might slip away from his grasp during the hours of darkness, and repeatedly during his restless night of the 17th Napoleon called for reports as to the position of the Allied army. His concern was unfounded. On the contrary, Wellington was defending on well known ground of his own choosing and was therefore at his most dangerous. With the promise of imminent help from his loyal Prussian ally, battle next day was assured, and the outcome far from certain for the French.

That night Napoleon was convinced Welling-ton had made a mistake, and considered that he was trapped with no hope of support. Had he known Wellington a little better he would not have been so optimistic. After starting the campaign at a strategic advantage, the French had by now thrown away and wasted nearly all of the benefits of their surprise and initiative at the start of the campaign, and Wellington had taken the campaign to prepared ground of his own choosing. If the Prussians arrived as promised, he could give Napoleon a very nasty surprise indeed.

18-19 JUNE:
THE BATTLE OF WAVRE

Wavre nestles in a lightly wooded valley, spanning the River Dyle by the two strong stone bridges that link the two halves of the town, the valley rising on either side to provide commanding artillery positions in the event of a defence. It was here that the main part of the Prussian army had finally halted, grateful of the reprieve from pursuit that had allowed it to elude the French grasp. Grouchy had indeed been late starting his pursuit on the 17th, Napoleon only releasing him at lunchtime. Even then, contact having been lost with the Prussians the night before, the leisurely pursuit had initially headed north-east from the battlefield towards Gembloux, not north towards Wavre.

By nightfall Grouchy's main force was camped around Gembloux itself, just seven miles north-east of the Ligny battlefield, with his advance cavalry strung out a few miles farther along the road, all heading north-east. He was already slightly east of the Prussian army, which was consolidating some twelve miles north and west of him behind the untouched IV Corps. Sloppy French reconnaissance had also completely missed a reinforced Prussian cavalry regiment positioned at Mont St. Gilbert, just six miles away to the north-west, and slightly behind his left, and it was only at 10 p.m. that night that the true location of the Prussian army at Wavre became known. The axis of pursuit was pivoted northwards the following day; Vandamme was ordered to begin the march north at 6 a.m. the next morning, Gérard following some two hours later. Tired after the fighting and marching of the previous days, the army was slow to start, giving the Prussians an extra two hours grace to begin their manoeuvres, time that was not to be wasted by Blücher's 'kinder', who by 8 a.m. were already widening the gap between the two forces.

The Prussian IV Corps under von Bülow was still intact, not having been engaged at Ligny. This fresh corps at least could be sent to Wellington's aid at Mont St. Jean, and Blücher was insistent that he would not break his word to Wellington to support him with at least two corps if the French gave him enough breathing space. Bulow's corps was at Dion le Mont, two miles south-east of Wavre itself, and it was ordered to move at 4 a.m. through II Corps (which was still south of the Dyle) through Wavre to Chapelle St. Lambert, and if the battle at Mont St. Jean had begun – but not otherwise – he was to attack the French right flank. Thus, by the time the French columns started out on the 18th, von Bülow was well on his way, reaching St. Lambert with his advance guard at around 10 a.m. But moving more or less through the remainder of the army, along a single road and through a crowded town, was at best a recipe for confusion and congestion. Even worse, a serious fire in Wavre slowed down the main body of IV Corps, and it was not until after midday that the main body arrived at St. Lambert.

As Bülow was struggling through the chaos of Wavre and the Prussian II Corps, Grouchy was unconcernedly getting ready to sit down to a late breakfast. It was 11.25 a.m. In the distance could be heard the rolling thunder of the first cannon fire from Napoleon's Grand Battery to the west, and Gérard and some other senior officers recommended that Grouchy should march to the sound of the guns and join the Emperor. It became a very heated discussion, and Gérard put his point in such a tactless and insulting manner that Grouchy took offence and insisted on keeping to his latest orders from the Emperor. These were rather poorly written and somewhat ambivalent, but they had clearly indicated the need to take possession of Wavre. He had no intention of invoking the notorious fury of the Corsican for disobeying orders, as Ney had already done in this campaign. Had Grouchy marched west at this point, he would almost certainly have intercepted the Prussian IV Corps under Bülow before it reached the field of Waterloo.

However, Grouchy had reasonable cause to be cautious about moving westward. He had actually sent a dispatch from Gembloux the previous night to appraise Napoleon of the Prussian threat, but no new orders had come. In point of fact his dispatch had reached the Emperor at around 2 a.m., where it was either forgotten or ignored, for it was not until 10 a.m. that Napoleon chose to issue orders to Grouchy, and these clearly indicated that his presence at Waterloo was not required. In any event, these orders were not to reach him until it was far too late for him to intervene at Waterloo.

Meanwhile, Prussian reconnaissance had put Grouchy's strength at about 20,000, mainly cavalry (it was, in fact, 33,000 including two infantry corps). Seeing that no attack was immediately developing, Pirch's II Corps was dispatched at about noon, and Ziethen's I Corps shortly after, adding to the total congestion and leaving just 15,000 men of Thielemann's III Corps to face Grouchy at the Dyle. Even these would have moved towards Waterloo if the congestion on the roads had not prevented it.

The unenthusiastic Bülow had assembled his corps around St. Lambert by about 3 p.m. Inexplicably he did not move to engage the French right flank as he had been ordered, but remained passively in full view of the battlefield below him. Perhaps he was resting his men before joining the battle, or expecting to be attacked as he moved through the nearby Bois de Paris; perhaps he was just waiting for II Corps to come up from the chaos behind him on the road; perhaps he was expecting hard-pressed Wellington to break before he could deploy. Whatever the reason, only the personal intervention and bullying of Blücher got him to move his leading brigades through the Bois de Paris to engage the French right, and when at 4 p.m. Bülow heard Grouchy's opening cannon fire to the east, he very nearly turned around again.

Back in Wavre, Grouchy opened the attack with a frontal assault by Vandamme on Wavre itself, which cleared the southern part of the town but which was frustrated at the bridges themselves.

A similar attempt by Hulot's brigade on a mill slightly south of the town was also beaten back, and, in an effort to secure a crossing of the Dyle, Grouchy diverted the remainder of Gérard's corps to Limale, two miles to the south-west, while the assault was renewed on the mill at Bierges. It was 5 p.m.

At Limale, Grouchy found a detachment of Ziethen's corps under Stengel – possibly left there by accident – defending the single bridge across the Dyle. The terrain favoured defence, but the superiority of numbers soon told, and the French had poured across the bridge and on to the high ground before darkness brought an end to the day's fighting.

▲General Friedrich Wilhelm von Bülow, Count Dennewitz (1755–1816) gives orders to an ADC; commander of Blücher's IV Corps in the Waterloo campaign, which led the Prussian army's arrival in support of

Wellington. Watercolour by Philip Heinrich Duncker. (ASKB)

The Battle of Wavre: Situation at 3.30pm 18 June

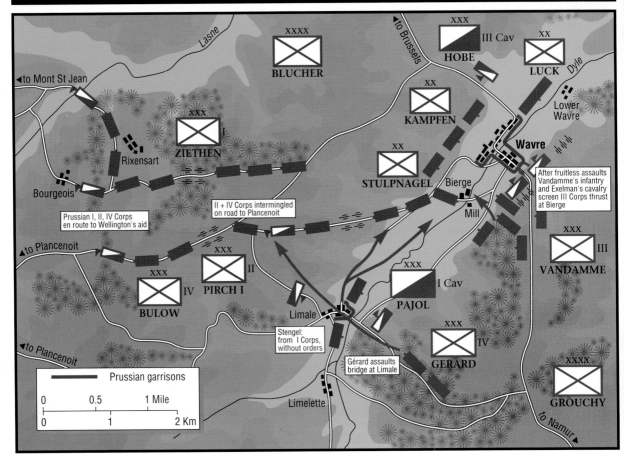

During the night a confused counter-attack was launched by Stülpnagel, but this was beaten off. Meanwhile Thielemann's appeals for help during the day had brought no reinforcements (indeed, during the night Stengel marched off quite without orders to rejoin his estranged corps). That night Thielemann received news as to the outcome of the fighting at Waterloo; but no such news reached Grouchy, and on the 19th the battle recommenced with the Prussians very thin on the ground. By 10 a.m., Thielemann had abandoned Wavre and retreated before overwhelming odds, the Prussian III Corps having tied down more than twice its own number for some 48 hours. But Grouchy's victory was short-lived, and at 10.30 the news from Waterloo reached him. Hearing that Pirch's Prussian II Corps was on its way to intercept him, he broke off and pulled back, eventually to France.

Tactically he had been the victor, but strategically he was beaten by a mixture of lethargy in his commanders, ambivalent orders, and an over-cautious lack of initiative on his own part. Once contact had been lost with the Prussians on the 17th, time was always going to be against the French, but even on the 18th a more vigorous thrust towards St. Lambert rather than Wavre would have reduced the number of Prussian corps available to aid Wellington and could have clinched the battle for Napoleon at Waterloo. In view of the events farther to the west, it is interesting to speculate what might have happened at both Waterloo and Wavre if the commanders of the two wings had been reversed, with the impulsive Ney following up the Prussians and the cautious but tactically precise Grouchy meeting Wellington.

18 JUNE: THE BATTLE OF WATERLOO

Waterloo Dawn

It was 2 a.m. before the Emperor received the dispatch that Grouchy had written at 10 p.m. the previous night. It stated that the Prussians appeared to have divided into three columns, and that he would infer from his current information that one portion of the army was moving on Wavre, presumably to join Wellington; one was heading to Liège, with Blücher himself; and a third, including the artillery, was en route for Namur. He had sent out a cavalry probe to determine precisely where the bulk of the Prussians were heading. If the mass of the Prussian army were making for Wavre, Grouchy intended to follow them, then act to keep them from Brussels and prevent them joining Wellington.

On the information he had available, Grouchy must have thought that a drive towards Wavre would push the remains of the shattered Prussian army north and east, away from Brussels, and keep them from their allies. Unfortunately for the French, Grouchy was at Gembloux when he wrote this, already slightly east of the Prussians, and, as a result of the delay in starting his pursuit from Ligny, the Prussian army before him was far from the broken army Napoleon expected him to find. Even as he was writing his dispatch, the Prussians were actually completing the concentration of all four corps around Wavre. Given that the Prussians had now regrouped, Grouchy's more easterly location, and the various delays in his setting out on the 18th, it is doubtful with hindsight whether Grouchy really had much chance of intercepting the Prussians as he intended. Without the benefit

▼ *Napoleon reviews the Grenadiers of the Imperial Guard on the morning of Waterloo; the civilian in custody of a cuirassier is presumably the local farmer Decoster, who Napoleon employed as a guide to the terrain. (Print after Ernest Crofts)*

◀ *The inn of La Belle Alliance, in the centre of the French position at Waterloo, reputedly (though perhaps not actually) the site of the meeting between Wellington and Blücher at the close of the action.*

of perfect knowledge, however, on the morning of the 18th Grouchy headed north to Wavre. It had turned 8 a.m. when he started, by which time the Prussians were already on their way to Wellington's aid.

As Grouchy's forces moved out, some miles away at Le Caillou, about a mile south of La Belle Alliance, Napoleon and his generals were sitting down to breakfast. The Emperor was in ebullient mood, and was counting on dinner in Brussels. He gave Soult short shrift when he tried to bring a note of realism into the after-breakfast meeting by suggesting that Napoleon should waste no time in recalling at least part of Grouchy's 34,000 men to help against Wellington. 'You think because Wellington defeated you that he must be a great general,' he retorted roughly. 'I tell you he is a bad general, that the English are poor troops, and that this affair will be no more serious than eating one's breakfast.'

In his turn, Reille suggested that the British infantry were impregnable to a frontal attack because of their firepower, and believed that manoeuvre was the key. Napoleon liked this even less, and broke up the meeting. Clearly an expensive frontal hammering in a bloody battle of attrition was to be ordered, with no time for the finesse of manoeuvre. As will be seen, both Soult and Reille gave advice that would probably have heralded victory later in the day, but in the unfounded optimism of Napoleon such experience was ignored. With a sweep of his hand, by avoiding a battle of manoeuvre, countless extra thousands were needlessly condemned to a violent and bloody death that day.

Once more in contrast to the Napoleon of earlier years, he was content to postpone the attack on the Allied lines for four hours to allow the ground to dry out a little, even though he had received several reports that the Prussians were coming to Wellington's aid. It would certainly make manoeuvring easier and quicker, especially for his artillery, which would also appreciate the firmer ground to increase the ricochet effects of their solid roundshot projectiles. This was actually a somewhat spurious argument, however, due to the fact that Wellington had clearly hidden most of his troops behind a ridge, out of artillery line of fire, which in turn negated the ricochet effect that the drier ground could offer. Perhaps Napoleon was merely rationalizing his delay in starting the battle, for his troops were well behind in their schedule for a 9 a.m. start – a situation unthinkable only a few years previously, as he himself had once said: 'Strategy is the art of making use of time and space. I am less chary of the latter than of the former; space we can recover, but time, never . . . I may lose a battle, but I shall never lose a minute.'

▶ *The rear wall of Hougoumont, its gate, and the chapel that stands in the compound; the scene of some of the fiercest fighting in the battle.*

Later events were to prove the four-hour delay a critical factor in the French defeat, with almost no compensating advantage to the French.

After scouting the battlefield and observing Wellington's visible dispositions, Napoleon went to Rossomme farm, about half a mile from La Belle Alliance, where at 10 a.m. he dictated his orders for the day and a dispatch to Grouchy that must have left him in no doubt that his presence at the field of Waterloo was not required, Grouchy actually being instructed to direct his movements on Wavre. Napoleon's battle plan was simple, uncomplicated and brutal. A frontal assault was to be made against Wellington's left centre by d'Erlon's I Corps, still totally intact from its lack of action on the 16th and keen to prove itself in the eyes of the Emperor. Napoleon was not to involve himself in the battle directly, but left the fine detail of the plan – and effective control – to a battle commander, Marshal Ney. Perhaps Ney's, performance in this campaign already should not have inspired such trust.

Even at this hour, before the battle had started, Napoleon had unwittingly sown the seeds of his own defeat. His relinquishing effective control to the rash Marshal Ney, his underestimation of the enemy in the face of experienced advice, his refusal to accept the possibility of Prussian reinforcement, his failure to recall Grouchy and his waste of a further four hours of the day were all to prove far-reaching and instrumental in his downfall. As we shall see, if just one of these factors had been changed, the fate of Wellington at Waterloo could well have been sealed. All would have been unthinkable of Napoleon in his prime.

The Battle Opens; d'Erlon's Assault

At about 11.25 the twenty-four 12-pounder cannon of the French batteries in front of d'Erlon's Corps thundered out against the Allied positions. Most of Wellington's infantry were behind the ridge, and the French cannon would have had to focus exclusively on thinning out the valuable and outnumbered Allied artillery opposite had not Bylandt's brigade been left exposed on the forward slopes, presumably accidentally.

Simultaneously, an attack was launched by Jérôme against Hougoumont, initially intended to be diversionary but in the event destined to last all day. Some 13,000 French were to be committed against just 2,000 British Guardsmen, who successfully beat off all attacks.

By 1 pm, the guns in front of d'Erlon had been joined by a further forty 6-pounders from I Corps, and another twenty-four 12-pounders from the Guard, making a massed battery of some 88 guns. These tore into the heart of Bylandt's exposed

53

The Battle of Waterloo, 18 June 1815: Initial Dispositions

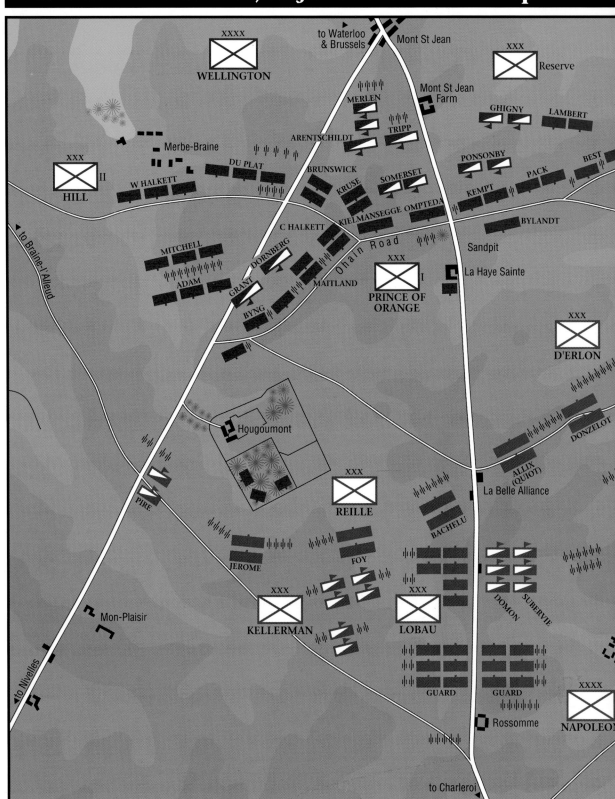

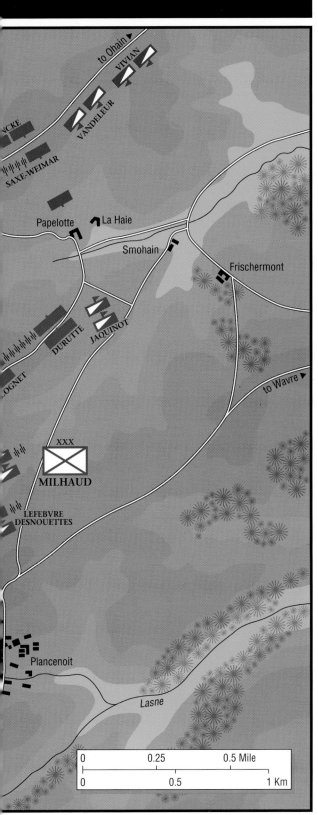

brigade, which was spared only the ricochet effect of near-misses in the still soggy ground.

At 1.30, even as the main attack began, a captured Prussian hussar was presented to the Emperor, and he confirmed that some 30,000 Prussians were on their way to support Wellington. To secure the French right, Lobau's corps was ordered to form a protective defence to the east of the main road, along with the cavalry of Domont and Subervie.

D'Erlon's I Corps advanced with the cuirassiers of Travers on its left, just east of the road, and those of Dubois to the west of the main road. The four divisions advanced in echelon, leading from the left, so that Allix's infantry would tie up the Allied centre in the area of La Haye Sainte while the main body of the attack swept past and up the hill, with Donzelot's troops then leading the assault. However, in the confusion so typical of war, the two central infantry divisions were drawn up in divisional column, rather than column of divisions. The former was a very unwieldy formation of 8 or 9 battalions drawn up densely with a full battalion frontage (200 files x 27 ranks); the latter were the more usual and far more flexible battalion columns, each with a frontage of two companies (70 men x 9 ranks) drawn up so as to leave room between battalions to allow deployment into line. As such, for most of the force involved in the main attack, there was room neither to deploy nor to manoeuvre when they reached their objectives, or in the event of a setback.

Few can have expected any setbacks after such a bombardment, and initially all went well for the French assault. The remaining Netherlanders broke before the advancing mass of more than 18,000 French infantry. Allix took the garden and orchard of La Haye Sainte, drove out the 95th from the gravel pit and pressed hard at Major Baring's Germans in the farmhouse itself. Travers' cuirassiers broke one of Ompteda's battalions sent to Baring's aid, and the remainder of the French swept past and advanced up the rapidly emptying slope. But the congestion in the French ranks was rapidly becoming unbearable as the uneven ground and the gradient pressed the files and ranks together into one amorphous mass. Donzelot's division, now leading the assault, halted below

◄ The defence of the woods and château of Hougoumont; the flank companies of the 2nd Battalion, 2nd (Coldstream) Guards (right and centre) repel an attack by Jérôme Bonaparte's 6th Division. (Painting by Denis Dighton)

◄ The interior of the yard at Hougoumont, defended by flank companies of British Foot Guards. (Print after Robert Hillingford).

◄ The death of Sir Thomas Picton at the head of his division at the height of the battle; he had been wounded quite severely at Quatre Bras but had concealed the fact so that he could retain his command at Waterloo. He is shown here wearing a staff officer's bicorn hat; in actual fact he wore his civilian 'round hat' instead. (Aquatint by S. Mitan after Captain George Jones)

the crest in order to try and deploy from his crowded formation.

Bylandt's Belgians may have bolted to the rear, but Picton's division was ready to rise to the challenge – quite literally. They had been lying down, sheltering from the French bombardment in the cover of the sunken road and the broken hedges at the top of the reverse slope. To Picton's cry of 'Rise up!', the 3,000 men of his division stood up to meet the anticipated assault. Then, with perfect timing, as Donzelot tried vainly to organize his chaotic mass of troops, Picton led Kempt's brigade forward to the crest, clearing a slight re-entrant in the ridge and sweeping the French tirailleur skirmishers before them. With a loud 'hurrah', a terrible fusillade from the brigade tore into the deploying column from less than 40 yards. The hail of bullets literally scythed down the leading ranks and added panic and terror to the confusion of the column beneath them. The French infantry wavered under the withering fire of some of the best trained infantry in the world; then, with a 'Charge! Hurrah!', Picton ordered the brigade forward with the bayonet to sweep the French from the hill. They were his final words.

As Kempt's brigade swept down the hill he fell, shot through the temple as the charge successfully threw back the whole of Donzelot's division. Examination of the body later also revealed a further wound that Picton had received at Quatre Bras, but which he had bravely not disclosed in spite of the pain it must have caused him.

Meanwhile Marcognet, catching up with Donzelot's deploying troops, did not stop below the crest to deploy but, sensing victory within his grasp, swept on over it in column with enthusiastic cries of 'Vive l'Empereur!'. It was to be short-lived elation. They rushed over the crest to find Pack's extended lines far overlapping the head of the column. On command the British let loose devastating close-range volleys that stopped the advancing column in its tracks.

On the crest, Marcognet had been halted but not routed. Farther down the hill Travers' cavalry

▼'Wellington at Waterloo': the Duke, in his customary civilian costume of blue frock-coat and cape and plain hat, gives orders to his staff, as the Life Guards of Somerset's brigade charge into action in the background. Painting by Abraham Cooper. (ASKB)

ANGLO- ⊠ ALLIED
WELLINGTON

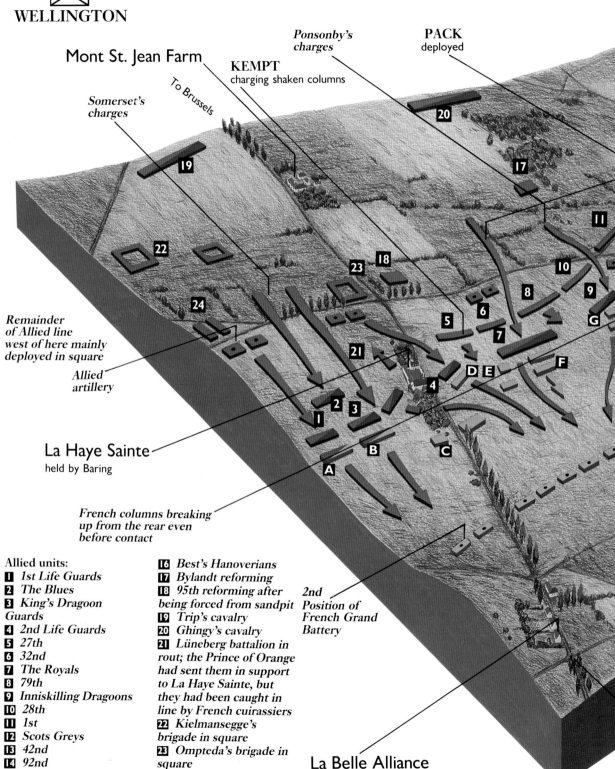

Ponsonby's charges

PACK
deployed

Mont St. Jean Farm

KEMPT
charging shaken columns

To Brussels

Somerset's charges

20

19

17

22

11

23

18

10

24

8

9

5

6

G

Remainder of Allied line west of here mainly deployed in square

7

21

D **E**

F

Allied artillery

4

2

3

1

B

C

La Haye Sainte
held by Baring

A

French columns breaking up from the rear even before contact

2nd
Position of
French Grand
Battery

Allied units:
1 *1st Life Guards*
2 *The Blues*
3 *King's Dragoon Guards*
4 *2nd Life Guards*
5 *27th*
6 *32nd*
7 *The Royals*
8 *79th*
9 *Inniskilling Dragoons*
10 *28th*
11 *1st*
12 *Scots Greys*
13 *42nd*
14 *92nd*
15 *44th*

16 *Best's Hanoverians*
17 *Bylandt reforming*
18 *95th reforming after being forced from sandpit*
19 *Trip's cavalry*
20 *Ghingy's cavalry*
21 *Lüneberg battalion in rout; the Prince of Orange had sent them in support to La Haye Sainte, but they had been caught in line by French cuirassiers*
22 *Kielmansegge's brigade in square*
23 *Ompteda's brigade in square*
24 *Halkett in column*

La Belle Alliance
Napoleon's forward HQ

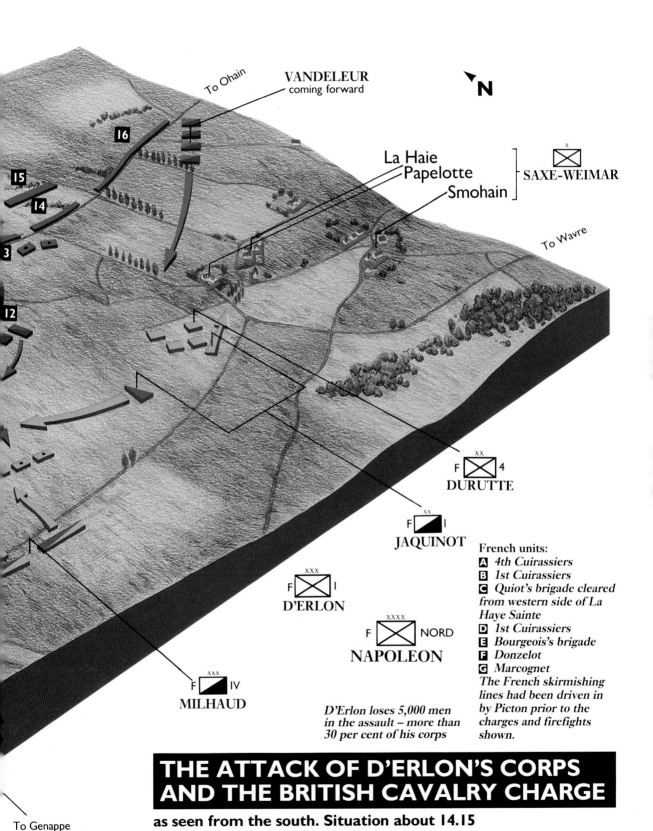

To Ohain

VANDELEUR
coming forward

N

16

15

14

3

12

La Haie
Papelotte
Smohain

SAXE-WEIMAR

To Wavre

F ⊠ 4
DURUTTE

F ◨ I
JAQUINOT

F ⊠ I
D'ERLON

French units:
A *4th Cuirassiers*
B *1st Cuirassiers*
C *Quiot's brigade cleared from western side of La Haye Sainte*
D *1st Cuirassiers*
E *Bourgeois's brigade*
F *Donzelot*
G *Marcognet*
The French skirmishing lines had been driven in by Picton prior to the charges and firefights shown.

F ⊠ NORD
NAPOLEON

F ◨ IV
MILHAUD

D'Erlon loses 5,000 men in the assault – more than 30 per cent of his corps

THE ATTACK OF D'ERLON'S CORPS AND THE BRITISH CAVALRY CHARGE

as seen from the south. Situation about 14.15

To Genappe

◀ *Sergeant Charles Ewart of the 2nd (Royal North British) Dragoons (Royal Scots Greys) (left centre) captures the 'Eagle' of the French 45th Ligne during the charge of the 'Union' Brigade, one of the most famous incidents in the battle. In actual fact the 2nd Dragoons wore oilskin covers over their fur caps on campaign, and their horse-furniture did not include holster-caps. Painting by Orlando Norie. (ASKB)*

◀ *The Earl of Uxbridge leads a cavalry charge against French cuirassiers; Uxbridge (centre) is shown in hussar uniform, which he wore at the battle – he was colonel of the 7th Queen's Own Light Dragoons (Hussars) – but the incident depicted appears to be unrecorded. (Painting by Orlando Norie. (ASKB)*

started to move forward against Kempt's now exposed brigade, picking their way through the throng, ready to press the British into squares for the infantry to finish off as they rallied, or else to ride them into the ground where they stood. Durutte's fresh division was also coming up on Marcognet's right. Outnumbered by nearly four to one, fully committed, with no reserves behind them, and with Picton himself dead, the Fifth Division was only minutes away from disaster.

In the very nick of time, the cavalry came to the rescue. Uxbridge had brought up the two brigades of British heavy cavalry. Somerset's brigade consisted of the 1st and 2nd Life Guards, Royal Horse Guards and 1st Dragoon Guards. The other, led by Ponsonby, consisted of the 1st Royal Dragoons, the 6th Dragoons, and the 2nd Dragoons; the grey horses of the latter had earned the regiment the nickname of 'The Greys'. This was perhaps the most carefully hoarded cavalry force in Europe, Wellington never having had the luxury of plentiful cavalry in his armies. As a result, the British heavies were superbly mounted on a quality of horse that had totally disappeared from the armies of continental Europe following the intensive campaigns of 1812 onwards. They were big men, on big horses, and with a total confidence that nothing could stand in their way.

With a perfect sense of timing, Uxbridge led his heavy cavalry against the stunned but recovering French. Somerset's brigade went to the west of the main road, Ponsonby's to the east. Somerset's cavalry met Dubois' cuirassiers just west of La Haye Sainte, the easternmost squadron of these cuirassiers being partly disordered in crossing the sunken road. Better mounted, the British routed them on contact, along with Allix's infantry that was pressing around the farm. However (and not for the first time) elements of the British cavalry got out of hand, failed to rally behind the reserve squadrons, and took their charge right on to the French Grand Battery.

Ponsonby attacked Donzelot and Marcognet in two lines – the Royals and Inniskillings in the first line, and the Scots Greys in reserve to their left and rear. The latter soon forgot their supporting role, however, and swept on into Marcognet's flanks to complete the total rout of this Division.

Supporting charges by Vandeleur's light brigade pressed Durutte back – in rather better order than the rest of the Corps – to complete a charge across the whole sector that was unstoppable. The French lost some 5,000 men and two eagles, and only on the extreme right at Papelotte and Frischermont did they meet with any measure of success at all.

But, not content with success against d'Erlon's infantry, the frenzied Greys also ignored the call to rally and swept up amongst the French battery where, the horses blown from the charge, they none the less set about sabring as many gunners as they could find. However, together with Somerset's remnants they were flung back with heavy losses by fresh cuirassiers and lancers. Only prompt action by Vandeleur's light horse allowed them the cover they needed in their escape.

It was now 3 p.m. A lull descended on the battle as both sides paused to regroup. The French attack had been broken up, but at a loss of some 40 per cent of Wellington's entire cavalry – and nearly all of it the heavy cavalry that would have been invaluable against the assaults that must surely follow. And follow they did. Napoleon, perhaps suspicious that he might have made a mistake in giving Ney so much control, now gave him a direct and categoric order that he must immediately take La Haye Sainte.

▲ *The Union Brigade overruns (but could not remove) a battery of French artillery: the cavalry with bearskin caps are members of the 2nd (Royal North British) Dragoons; those with maned helmets are members of the 1st (Royal) or 6th (Inniskilling) Dragoons. (Print after W. B. Wollen)*

▼ *One of the most famous members of the British Army, Captain Edward Kelly of the 1st Life Guards, right, in combat with a French cuirassier; one of his exploits was the killing of a cuirassier officer, whose epaulettes he was reputed to have removed as trophies. This print published by Thomas Kelly shows the old pattern of helmet, replaced by a version with worsted comb, which was worn at the battle.*

Ponsonby's Union Brigade; 1, Officer, 1st Royal Dragoons, service dress; 2, Trooper, and North British Dragoons (The Scots Greys), service dress; 3, Corporal, 6th (Inniskilling) Dragoons, Marching Order. (Bryan Fosten)

The French Cavalry Attack

A little before 4 p.m. Ney took Quiot's and Donzelot's brigades from the rallied remainder of I Corps against La Haye Sainte but found that Baring's position had been reinforced. The attack was repulsed in just a few minutes, but while at the front, Ney saw some British battalions still returning to the cover of the reverse slopes, and further 'columns' of wounded heading back towards Mont St. Jean. Taking these to be retreating troops, he immediately ordered up a brigade of Milhaud's cuirassiers to press the perceived retreat into a rout. Somehow the attack escalated in all the excitement, and instead of just a brigade of cuirassiers, some 5,000 French cavalry of all types – many without orders – were suddenly moving against the Allied right centre. On the ridge Wellington and his staff were amazed that such a mistake could have been made. Wellington ordered his troops into square and advanced some of the squares to just behind the Allied cannon lining the crest, so that the gunners could run back into the shelter of the squares at the last minute and then quickly return to the guns in the expectation that the unsupported cavalry would be beaten back.

The French cavalry advanced spectacularly, *en echelon* from the right. Funnelled into the gap between La Haye Sainte and Hougoumont, charging uphill, through high corn and over soggy ground, it is not surprising that the attack was delivered barely at a trot, and the Allied gunners lost no time in taking full advantage of the superb target opportunity before them. Whole files were destroyed by the crashing roundshot flying through the crowded mass of horses and riders, while repeated charges of shell and shrapnel emptied many saddles in the rear ranks. Then it was down to canister range, where whole ranks would disappear at a stroke, the following horses stumbling over the broken carnage that was once some of the finest cavalry in Europe. And still they came on. Disordered by the mounds of corpses and wreckage, the sunken road and the ceaseless fire of steady infantry, wave after wave of this magnificent arm broke itself ineffectually against the squares, to be thrown back down the hill, where, reforming with others similarly repulsed, they would again launch their charge into the very mouths of the re-manned cannon they had just passed, and to the infantry behind.

No less than four assaults took place on the Allied squares by this cavalry, in some places supported by horse batteries, but otherwise without any support or coordination. Advancing French infantry could have approached unmolested by artillery fire as the Allied gunners sheltered within the squares from the milling horsemen, but the opportunity was missed. 'That premature movement may have a fatal effect on the fortunes of the day. It is too early by an hour,' grumbled Napoleon to Soult. 'He has compromised us, as he did at Jena,' came the reply.

◀ *French cavalry assail a British square; note the temporarily abandoned artillery, the gunners being ordered to shelter inside the squares until the French cavalry retired, with a wheel removed from the gun to prevent its being dragged away by the French during the attack.*

▲ *The 28th (North Gloucestershire) Regiment, formed in square, repelling an attack by French cuirassiers at Waterloo. The regiment was especially distinguished by its* retention of the old 'stovepipe' shako, with distinctive badge, which had been replaced for the remainder of the line infantry by the false-fronted 1812-pattern shako. (Print after W. B. Wollen)

▼ *French cavalry charge British squares at Waterloo; La Haye Sainte appears in mid-ground centre, and Wellington in mid-ground right. Rockets fired by Whinyates' battery are* conspicuous in the sky. Aquatint by R. Reeve after William Heath. (ASKB)

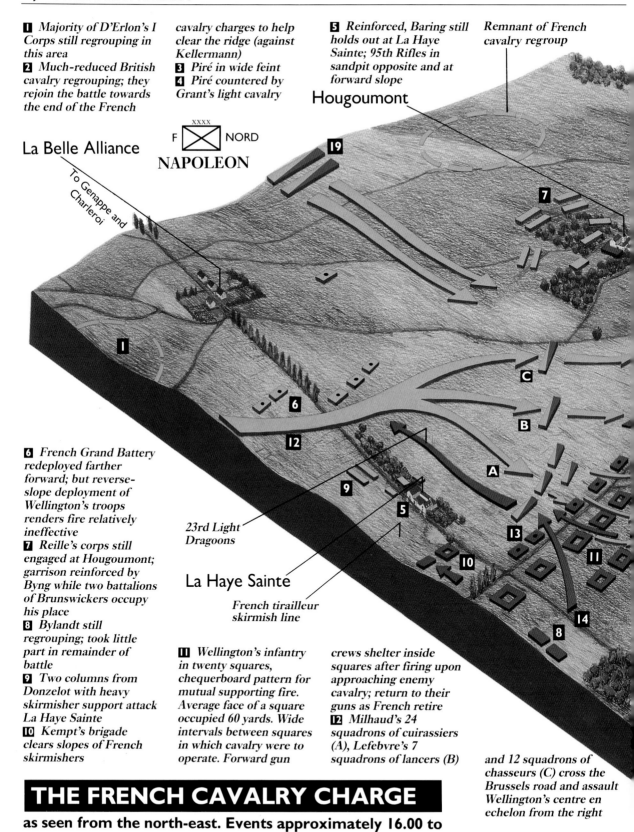

1 Majority of D'Erlon's I Corps still regrouping in this area

2 Much-reduced British cavalry regrouping; they rejoin the battle towards the end of the French cavalry charges to help clear the ridge (against Kellermann)

3 Piré in wide feint

4 Piré countered by Grant's light cavalry

5 Reinforced, Baring still holds out at La Haye Sainte; 95th Rifles in sandpit opposite and at forward slope

Remnant of French cavalry regroup

Hougoumont

La Belle Alliance

To Genappe and Charleroi

F ⊠ NORD
XXXX
NAPOLEON

6 French Grand Battery redeployed farther forward; but reverse-slope deployment of Wellington's troops renders fire relatively ineffective

7 Reille's corps still engaged at Hougoumont; garrison reinforced by Byng while two battalions of Brunswickers occupy his place

8 Bylandt still regrouping; took little part in remainder of battle

9 Two columns from Donzelot with heavy skirmisher support attack La Haye Sainte

10 Kempt's brigade clears slopes of French skirmishers

23rd Light Dragoons

La Haye Sainte

French tirailleur skirmish line

11 Wellington's infantry in twenty squares, chequerboard pattern for mutual supporting fire. Average face of a square occupied 60 yards. Wide intervals between squares in which cavalry were to operate. Forward gun crews shelter inside squares after firing upon approaching enemy cavalry; return to their guns as French retire

12 Milhaud's 24 squadrons of cuirassiers (A), Lefebvre's 7 squadrons of lancers (B) and 12 squadrons of chasseurs (C) cross the Brussels road and assault Wellington's centre en echelon from the right

THE FRENCH CAVALRY CHARGE

as seen from the north-east. Events approximately 16.00 to 18.00

13 French cavalry face seven batteries as they advance

14 1st Dutch Belgians counter-charge French

cuirassiers; 23rd Light Dragoons support them by striking cuirassiers on the flank before pursuing across valley and into the batteries behind. This is the only recorded

instance of Dutch cavalry charging; however, they leave the field on being ordered to charge a second time

15 French cavalry break around the squares in

face of artillery and musket fire. Disordered, they are picked upon by small units of British and KGL cavalry and thrown back on to the muskets of the infantry

16 Much movement at Wellington's right-centre as French units are disordered by the squares and charged by British/ KGL cavalry, who pursue them over the crest before being repulsed in turn as the French rally

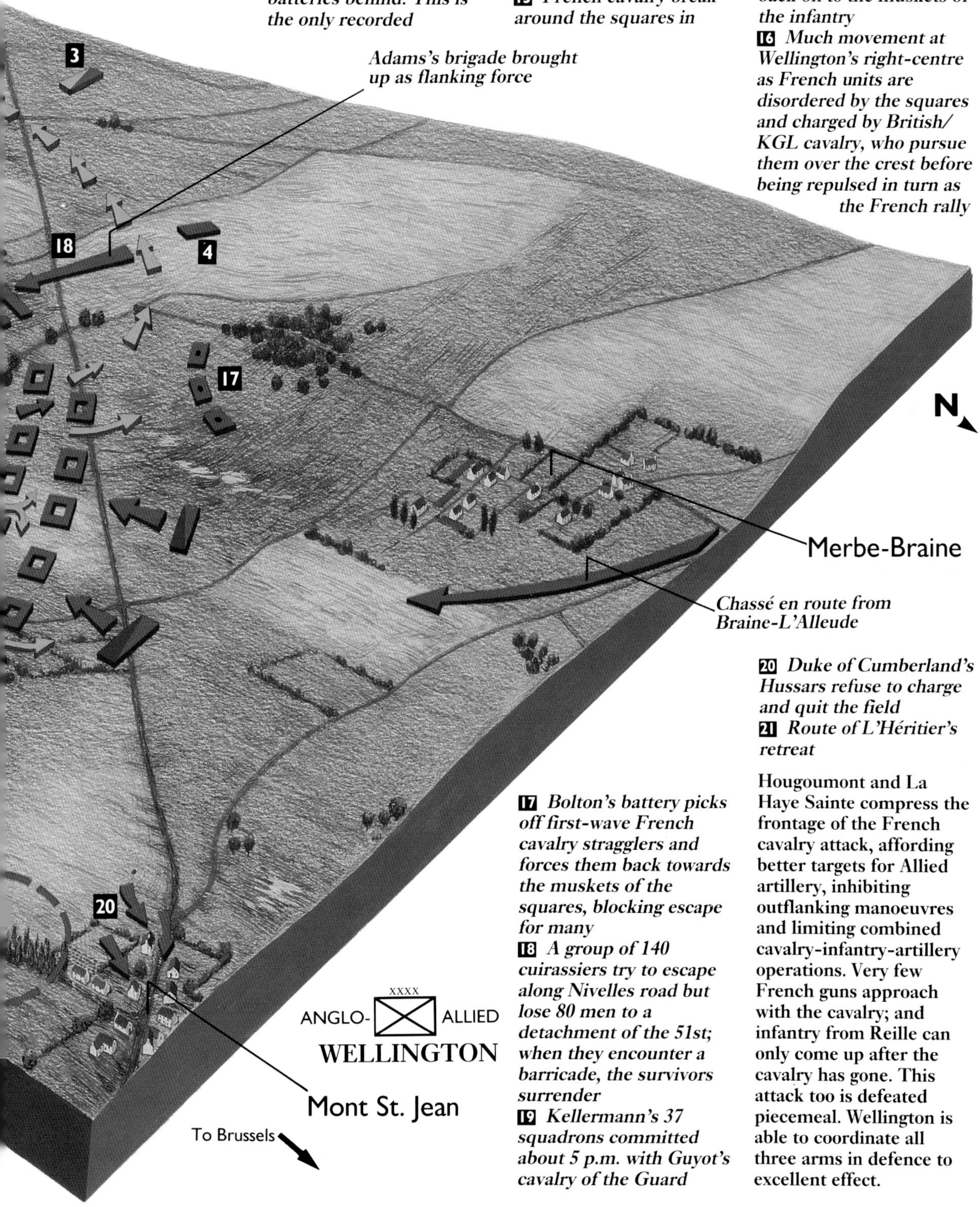

Adams's brigade brought up as flanking force

Merbe-Braine

Chassé en route from Braine-L'Alleude

20 Duke of Cumberland's Hussars refuse to charge and quit the field

21 Route of L'Héritier's retreat

17 Bolton's battery picks off first-wave French cavalry stragglers and forces them back towards the muskets of the squares, blocking escape for many

18 A group of 140 cuirassiers try to escape along Nivelles road but lose 80 men to a detachment of the 51st; when they encounter a barricade, the survivors surrender

19 Kellermann's 37 squadrons committed about 5 p.m. with Guyot's cavalry of the Guard

Hougoumont and La Haye Sainte compress the frontage of the French cavalry attack, affording better targets for Allied artillery, inhibiting outflanking manoeuvres and limiting combined cavalry-infantry-artillery operations. Very few French guns approach with the cavalry; and infantry from Reille can only come up after the cavalry has gone. This attack too is defeated piecemeal. Wellington is able to coordinate all three arms in defence to excellent effect.

ANGLO- ⊠ ALLIED
WELLINGTON

Mont St. Jean

To Brussels

N

By 5 p.m. fully 10,000 horsemen had been fed into the maelstrom in an attempt to help extricate the first, blown assaults, yet still no infantry had come up in support, nor any spiking equipment to silence the Allied guns. Although casualties mounted within the British squares, they were able to stand firm while there was no threat from the French infantry, and some well timed charges by the Allied light cavalry and the remnant of the heavy cavalry helped to clear the now tiring French horsemen from the hill. All had been repulsed when, at last, at 5.30 p.m., 8,000 infantry from Reille's corps finally arrived in support. It was too late for the tired horsemen now regrouping in the lee of the ridge. Lord Hill's infantry swung out on the Allied right towards Hougoumont to allow converging fire on the French infantry as they came up the slope. In view of the presence of cavalry still in the area, Wellington's infantry had formed reinforced (four-deep) lines to meet the threat but still gave such a volume of fire that within ten minutes they had broken the attack and inflicted more than 20 per cent losses on the columns.

The second major assault on the Allied lines had been broken. And now at last the Prussians were making their presence felt on the French right.

The Prussians Arrive

Wellington had expected the two Prussian Corps dispatched from Wavre to reinforce his right wing by lunchtime, and he had left space in his deployment behind Picton to allow for their arrival. But muddles in Prussian staff work caused confusion on the march as the long columns converged, and the sticky mud slowed progress to a crawl. As a result, the first corps to arrive, Bülow's IV Corps, only came into action shortly after 4 p.m. The first brigades had emerged from the Bois de Paris on the far right of the French, and behind d'Erlon's corps, while the remainder of the column was strung out way to the rear because of the long march over difficult ground.

As the Prussians came out of the wood, they met Lobau's corps formed up at right-angles to the French main line, linking up with Durutte on the French right. Lobau attacked before the Prussians could deploy fully, pushing Bülow back on the wood, but a Prussian thrust towards Plancenoit threatened to turn Lobau's right and recovered the situation. By 5 p.m., with the arrival of Pirch's II Corps on Bülow's left, Plancenoit was threatened from three sides, and Lobau's corps was in definite difficulties. Vicious fighting broke out on the edge of the village, where the Prussians retained a foothold, and Prussian reserves were coming up to exploit it against the beleaguered French. A division of the Young Guard came to their aid and briefly secured Plancenoit before fresh waves of Prussian assaults wrested it from their grasp in a bloody hand-to-hand struggle. The Young Guard was repulsed and Lobau's thinning and tired lines were being relentlessly pressed back. If only Grouchy had been there. . . .

Things were looking decidedly tight for Napoleon by now, and with his front line engaged all along its length there was only the Guard left to reinforce his wavering right. If Plancenoit were not retaken, his entire flank could collapse. He sent two battalions of the Old Guard to take Plancenoit itself and lined up the remaining eleven battalions along the main road, facing east. Lobau's hard pressed corps in turn shortened its lines and moved north-east of Plancenoit. The demonstration and threat of the Old Guard was in itself nearly enough. The two battalions stormed through Plancenoit in a brilliant counter-attack, which flung a full fourteen battalions of Prussians back from the immediate area of the village and bolstered the sagging morale of the French right wing. Within the hour, the line had been stabilized; each side paused to regroup forces and recover strength.

Bringing most of the Old Guard back into the central reserve at around 7 p.m., Napoleon must have felt that victory was still within his grasp, for, while he had been preoccupied on his right with the Prussians, Ney had remained highly active in the centre.

Wellington's Crisis

Still determined to take La Haye Sainte, the key to the battle, Ney had set up a third assault on the

▲Blücher encourages his army in their march to Wellington's relief at Waterloo; the Prussian commander wears his service uniform of a caped greatcoat and peaked Mütze (field cap). (Print after R. Eichstädt)

▼'Schlacht bei Waterloo am 18 Juni 1815'; a watercolour by Philip Heinrich Duncker showing the advance of Prussian infantry, apparently opposed by French troops wearing bearskin caps (left mid-ground) and carrying two 'Eagles', presumably Chasseurs à Pied of the Imperial Guard defending Plancenoit. (ASKB)

▼ *King's German Legion: 1, Sergeant, Sharpshooters, Light Company, 3rd Line Battalion; 2, Officer, Grenadier Company, 1st Line Battalion; 3, Private, Light Company, 2nd Line Battalion. These battalions were all part of the 1st Brigade of the Second Division commanded by Clinton. (Bryan Fosten)*

Allied centre. Launched a little before 6 p.m., this time the attack was set up properly, using combined arms of infantry, cavalry and artillery in the assault. Many of the Allied troops were forced into square by the presence of the enemy cavalry, seriously reducing the number of muskets that could bear on the approaching French infantry. Worse, supporting French artillery cut large holes in the densely packed formations, who could only close ranks in the face of the combined arms assault.

The pressure on Wellington's army was now almost intolerable. Although the line had held all afternoon, casualties had not been light, and streams of wounded had flooded back to the rear. Desertion was not unknown, even in the generally dependable British ranks, and some units – such as the Duke of Cumberland's Hussars – had left the field *en masse*. The staying-power of the Belgian troops was very questionable by now, and Brialmont described the road to Brussels as being so crowded with fugitives that Wellington had no choice but to hold his ground.

Wellington's centre was rapidly thinning under the intense pressure of Ney's third attack. General

▲ *The light battalions of the King's German Legion attempted to hold La Haye Sainte with bayonet and rifle-butt after their ammunition had been used; lack of ammunition alone caused the post to be evacuated after a most heroic defence. (Print after W. B. Wollen)*

▼ *The Prince of Orange directs Dutch troops in opposition to the French to the right of La Haye Sainte: a crucial stage in the Battle of Waterloo at the height of one of the French attacks, shortly before the Prince was wounded and carried from the field. Painting by Charles Warren. (ASKB)*

◀ *The defence of La Haye Sainte: the light infantry of the King's German Legion, commanded by Major George Baring, attempt to repel the final French assault. (Painting by Adolf Northen)*

◀ *Napoleon observes the battle from a position at the rear of the Grenadiers of the Imperial Guard, recognisable by their bearskin caps and their painted fabric cartridge-box covers; a superbly emotive lithograph after Auguste Raffet. (ASKB)*

Ompteda fell dead near the high road; Sir William Delancey received a mortal wound from a cannon-ball as he rode next to Wellington; Sir Alexander Gordon received his death wound nearby; farther to the right, the Prince of Orange and General Alten were struck down.

Kielmansegge's tough Germans were at last pushed back in the centre, leaving a yawning gap in the Allied line. Worse still, by being locked up in squares for most of the afternoon during the French cavalry attack, command control over most of the battlefield had been severed, with the result that the garrison of La Haye Sainte had been neither reinforced nor resupplied. Baring's men there, heavily depleted and having fired their last rounds, had no alternative but to fight their way out and rejoin the main lines. Of the original 400 defenders of the farm, only 42 got out.

Taking La Haye Sainte at last, Ney wasted no time in positioning an artillery battery there, which enfiladed the Allied troops at less than 300 yards' range. All Wellington could do was to call in his last reserves from the extreme left and extreme right to plug the rapidly widening gap in the centre.

'Le centre est ouvert! Vive l'Empereur!'

Now was the time for Ney to launch one last assault to break through Wellington's decimated centre. But what with? His own force was stretched, engaged all along the front, and like Wellington he had no reserves in the immediate area. He needed reinforcements, perhaps from the Guard. He sent Colonel Héymès to ask the Emperor for more troops. When he arrived at the Emperor's observation post, Napoleon was himself under pressure on the right and was still preoccupied with his problems at Plancenoit. The Guard was strung out along the right flank in support of Lobau, and nothing more could be released to this wasteful Marshal. 'More troops!' raged Napoleon; 'Where am I to get them? Does he expect me to make them?'

Ney's reinforcements were not to come. The timing would have been critical, before Wellington's final reserves came up. The wavering line held as Chassé arrived from the far right, Wincke

from the far left, and Wellington himself brought up the raw and uncertain Brunswickers from the reserve to fill the gap. To keep the Brunswickers in place he lined up behind them Somerset and Ponsonby's cavalry brigades – brigades in name only, for between them they were barely two squadrons strong. His last reserves had been committed, the French had been checked for the time being, but where were the promised Prussians? 'Give me Blücher . . . or give me night . . .' was his quiet prayer. Had he but known it, in diverting Napoleon's final reserve the Prussian attacks on Plancenoit had probably already saved his army. It was 7 p.m.

The Assault by The Imperial Guard

Shortly after 7 p.m. the French right wing had been propped up sufficiently to pull most of the Old Guard back into reserve. The French position looked strong from La Belle Alliance. To the far right, Durutte held La Haye and Papelotte, with skirmishers thrown forward to the crest of the ridge; the rest of I Corps was busily engaged well

▲ 'The Interior of Hougoumont': the British Foot Guards defending Hougoumont charge to eject those French troops who penetrated by the rear gate. This engraving by T. Sutherland greatly overestimates the numbers of Frenchmen who forced their way into the interior of Hougoumont; the flames in the background stop before the chapel (right) is destroyed. (ASKB)

forward on the slopes to the right of La Haye Sainte, and at the farm itself the French cannon and sharpshooters were raking the Allied lines to right and left. Ney had breasted the ridge to the left of the road, and Wellington's lines showed considerable gaps. Wellington had clearly committed all his reserves, and since Ney's appeals half an hour before he must be even weaker. A supreme effort all along the front was called for, with an attack by the Imperial Guard to smash right through the centre and roll up the line – and there could still be enough time to tackle the Prussians before dark.

But even as the attack was being prepared, it became clear that the vision of success before him was illusory, for to the French right the blue uniforms of the Prussian I Corps could now be

▼ *The Imperial Guard:*
1, Sergeant, Grenadiers,
campaign dress;
2, Officer, Grenadiers,
campaign dress;
3, Sergeant-major,
Chasseurs, undress;
4, Chasseur, marching
order. (Bryan Fosten)

distinguished in the distance as they belatedly arrived at Smohain and Frischermont to link the two armies. Signs of panic were already starting to be seen on the French right as they speculated on the disaster that would follow. Only a supreme effort could save the day.

Ever ready to take a risk, as the Guard advanced Napoleon deliberately spread the news that the blue uniforms in the distance belonged to Grouchy's force. It gave his weary lines the strength to make a final effort, and, at last, here was the Guard, marching steadily on to break Wellington's line. It's use had always heralded the victorious end to a battle – victory was near; success was certain; the Guard had never been defeated. 'La Garde au feu! Voila Grouchy! Vive l'Empereur!'

Details of the actual attack are still slightly confused, with differing sources offering varying interpretations. However, it seems that of the fourteen battalions of the Guard, two were already committed at Plancenoit, which left twelve battalions available to the Emperor. Leaving three near La Belle Alliance, Napoleon himself led the remainder in column along the main Brussels road.

The Guard descended into the valley. Keeping three battalions there with him, Napoleon halted near La Belle Alliance and released the other six to Marshal Ney for the assault on the Allied centre. Most sources reveal that the assault went forward in battalion columns with a two-company wide frontage, but General Petit of the Imperial Guard, who helped Ney organize the attack, insists that a hollow square formation was used. Whatever the truth, it is probable that one of the six battalions was posted at the main road south of La Haye Sainte as the other five ascended the slope *en echelon*, the Grenadiers of the Middle Guard leading from the right, and with a pair of cannon in each interval. D'Erlon's battered I Corps launched a supporting attack to their right, while Reille should have provided some support from his easternmost battalions, but by some error these failed to materialize, leaving the Guard to advance alone, but confident.

Had the attack been made just half an hour earlier, the centre would have been open. As it

was, the leading battalion – the 1/3rd Grenadiers of the Middle Guard – crested the slope to be met by the Brunswickers and the remains of the British 30th and 73rd. The Grenadiers pushed them back, the Brunswickers breaking and Wellington himself riding to rally them. Chassé, behind them, had brought up van der Smissen's Dutch battery, which had fired on the Guard with good effect, and he then ordered up his two infantry brigades to plug the gap left by the Brunswickers. The sight of the Guard was enough for d'Aubreme's brigade, who promptly left the field in disorder. Ditmer's brigade, however, formed up on the left of the rallying 30th and 73rd British and charged the Grenadiers in fine order to hold the line.

Meanwhile the second echelon of the Imperial Guard, comprising the single battalion of the 4th Grenadiers, came up on the left of the 1/3rd and engaged in hand-to-hand combat with Colin Halkett's brigade, who were still in four-deep line. The line almost broke under the impact, but just held, Colin Halkett himself rallying the 33rd by seizing one of the colours, before falling himself.

▶ *At the critical point of the attack of the Imperial Guard, the Duke of Wellington orders the British Foot Guards to oppose them; the traditional exclamation 'Up Guards, and at them' was probably in actual fact 'Stand up, Guards' (they had been lying down to minimize the effect of artillery fire) and, to their commander, 'Now Maitland, now's your time!'. Wellington here (centre) gives the order; the Guards wear their service dress with covered shakos, and the French column appears in the background. Lithograph after John Augustus Atkinson. (ASKB)*

The fate of these two mêlées still hung in the balance when the third and fourth echelons arrived together in one mass, consisting of the 1st and 2nd Battalions of the 3rd Chasseurs. There was nothing to their front as they neared the road, until Wellington's voice called out clearly above the sounds of battle – 'Now Maitland, now's your time!' Then the order, 'Stand up, Guards!' The Duke had ordered all troops to lie down or shelter behind cover when under fire but not actually engaged, and Maitland's brigade of Guards had been lying down in the shelter of the banks of the road. The fifteen hundred Guards rose, it seemed, from the very ground just fifty yards in front of the French. Still in four ranks, they pounded the Chasseurs with rolling volleys that devastated the head of the attack at point-blank range. The attack wavered in disorder.

Almost without pausing for breath, the Guards charged the confused mass of the Chasseurs and threw them down the hill in rout. Near the bottom of the slope the pursuing and disordered Guards ran into the French fifth echelon, comprising the 4th Chasseurs, before breaking off and running back in double-quick time and considerable disorder to the crest between Halkett's and Adams' brigades, where they hastened to form up before the advancing Chasseurs.

As this was happening, Adams' brigade had not been idle. Colborne had wheeled the 52nd forward to take the last echelon of the Imperial Guard in flank as it came up the slope and halted it suddenly short of the ridge. A fierce fire-fight lasted for four minutes and cost 150 casualties in the 52nd alone, perhaps suggesting from the volume of return fire that the Chasseurs were indeed in hollow square formation at the time. Nevertheless the superior firepower of the British soldiers took its toll on the 4th Chasseurs and ripped the formation apart without mercy before they charged in with the bayonet.

The attack had been halted all along the front. In the valley, Napoleon was preparing to bring up a further three battalions of the Guard – 1st Chasseurs, 2nd Grenadiers and 2nd Chasseurs – when, looking up to the crest, his astonishment

Allied units:
1 Best
2 Kempt
3 Perponcher
4 Lambert, brought up from Mont St. Jean about 3.30 p.m.
5 Pack
6 Vincke
7 Merlen
8 Remnants of British heavy brigades
9 Ghingy
10 Vivian's cavalry arriving from left wing
11 Trip
12 Vivian (part)
13 Ompteda, Kruse, Brunswick, much reduced
14 C. Halkett, pushed back by Imperial Guard
15 Chassé
16 Maitland
17 Adams wheels forward to engage chasseurs in flank

ANGLO-⊠ALLIED
WELLINGTON

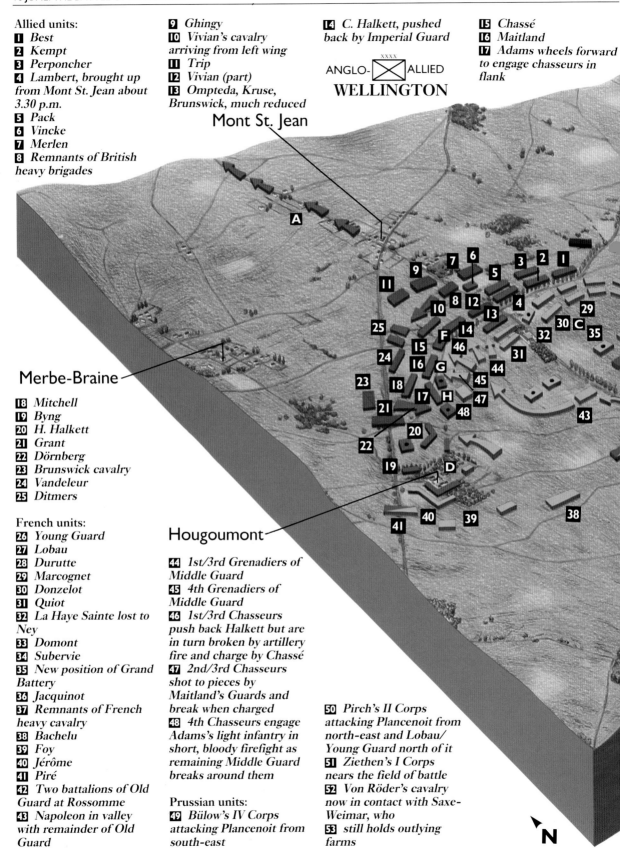

Mont St. Jean

Merbe-Braine

18 Mitchell
19 Byng
20 H. Halkett
21 Grant
22 Dörnberg
23 Brunswick cavalry
24 Vandeleur
25 Ditmers

French units:
26 Young Guard
27 Lobau
28 Durutte
29 Marcognet
30 Donzelot
31 Quiot
32 La Haye Sainte lost to Ney
33 Domont
34 Subervie
35 New position of Grand Battery
36 Jacquinot
37 Remnants of French heavy cavalry
38 Bachelu
39 Foy
40 Jérôme
41 Piré
42 Two battalions of Old Guard at Rossomme
43 Napoleon in valley with remainder of Old Guard

Hougoumont

44 1st/3rd Grenadiers of Middle Guard
45 4th Grenadiers of Middle Guard
46 1st/3rd Chasseurs push back Halkett but are in turn broken by artillery fire and charge by Chassé
47 2nd/3rd Chasseurs shot to pieces by Maitland's Guards and break when charged
48 4th Chasseurs engage Adams's light infantry in short, bloody firefight as remaining Middle Guard breaks around them

Prussian units:
49 Bülow's IV Corps attacking Plancenoit from south-east

50 Pirch's II Corps attacking Plancenoit from north-east and Lobau/Young Guard north of it
51 Ziethen's I Corps nears the field of battle
52 Von Röder's cavalry now in contact with Saxe-Weimar, who
53 still holds outlying farms

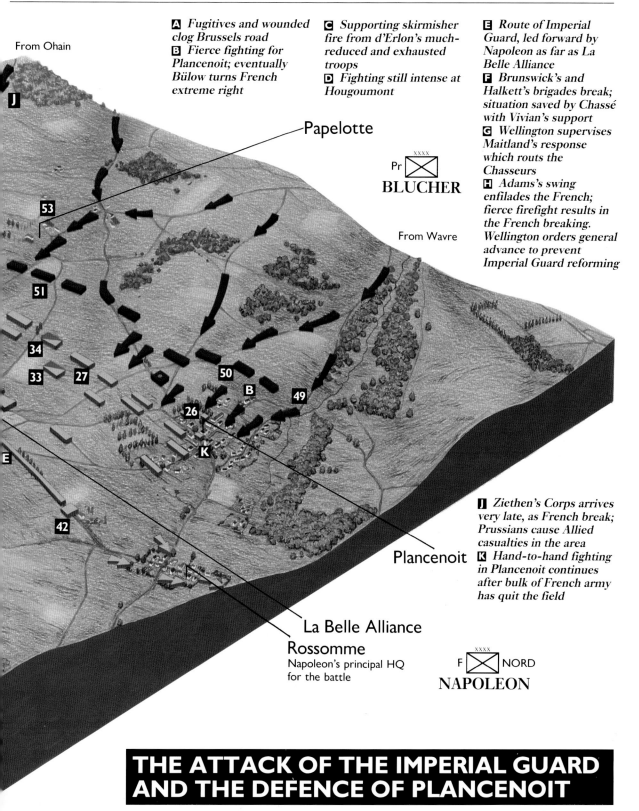

From Ohain

A Fugitives and wounded clog Brussels road
B Fierce fighting for Plancenoit; eventually Bülow turns French extreme right

C Supporting skirmisher fire from d'Erlon's much-reduced and exhausted troops
D Fighting still intense at Hougoumont

E Route of Imperial Guard, led forward by Napoleon as far as La Belle Alliance
F Brunswick's and Halkett's brigades break; situation saved by Chassé with Vivian's support
G Wellington supervises Maitland's response which routs the Chasseurs
H Adams's swing enfilades the French; fierce firefight results in the French breaking. Wellington orders general advance to prevent Imperial Guard reforming

Papelotte

Pr XXXX
BLUCHER

From Wavre

J Ziethen's Corps arrives very late, as French break; Prussians cause Allied casualties in the area
K Hand-to-hand fighting in Plancenoit continues after bulk of French army has quit the field

Plancenoit

La Belle Alliance

Rossomme
Napoleon's principal HQ for the battle

F XXXX NORD
NAPOLEON

THE ATTACK OF THE IMPERIAL GUARD AND THE DEFENCE OF PLANCENOIT

as seen from the south-west. The final all-out assault by the French to coincide with the attack by the Middle Guard

◄ *Light Dragoons of the King's German Legion (left mid-ground) charge a regiment of French lancers; an incident presumably towards the end of the battle of Waterloo when the KGL Light Dragoons advanced towards Colbert's lancer brigade of Subervie's 5th Cavalry Division. The French are depicted in Polish-style costume, although the French Chevau-Léger-Lanciers in the campaign wore crested helmets. Painting by Charles Warren. (ASKB)*

must have been absolute. 'Mais, ils sont mêlées!'

Even as he spoke, the rearward movement of his Guard was evident. The entire attack had been repelled. The perfect formations of just a few minutes before were now a single confused blue mass, highlighted with the glint of slashing steel as Vivian's and Vandeleur's light cavalry hacked within its midst. The impossible had happened. The invincible had been vanquished. A great, incredible sob sped along the French lines – 'La Garde recule! Sauve qui peut!'

To the right, the blue coats seen at Smohain were now nearer, their artillery firing on the French lines. Could this be Grouchy firing? There had always been considerable suspicion of the Bourbon troops under his control. Had he defected to the Bourbons? 'Traison!' came the cry, 'Nous sommes trahis!' Soon, even in the deepening gloom of twilight, they were clearly seen as Prussians, not Grouchy's force. The army had indeed been betrayed.

Seeing the moment was ripe, Wellington raised his cocked hat forward to signal a general advance.

◄ *Wellington orders the advance, while a British cavalryman brings a captured French 'Eagle' as a trophy. This watercolour by John Augustus Atkinson also depicts the carnage and suffering – ignored by many artists.*

The hussar officer in front of Wellington is the Earl of Uxbridge. (ASKB)

▼ *The leading elements of the Prussian army storm into the blazing wreck of Plancenoit, still held valiantly by the French*

defenders. This provides an excellent illustration of the Prussian infantry's campaign uniform, with their most distinctive, oilskin-covered shakos. (Painting by Adolf Northen)

The army descended the slopes, as the French army crumbled before it. In the valley, only Reille's corps on the left and the three battalions of the Old Guard at La Belle Alliance held fast to offer a last chance of a rallying point for the fleeing army. It was to no avail. Plancenoit was again taken by the Prussians, driving all before them towards the main road in their pursuit. Only when Napoleon saw that all was lost did he leave the field. The squares of the Guard finally broke up after taking musket fire in the face of overwhelming odds, and their commander, General Cambronne, surrendered to Colonel H. Halkett. At 10 p.m. Wellington and Blücher met at La Belle Alliance, where Blücher offered to take up the pursuit. This was gratefully accepted by Wellington, whose troops had by then been fighting for more than ten hours.

It had indeed been 'a damned near-run thing', but the steadiness and order of the British trained troops had sustained Wellington's line right to the end. To Napoleon's dismay, Reille's prediction

◀ 'The flight of Napoleon from Waterloo': Napoleon and his aides leave the battlefield as the French army disintegrates in the background. Engraving by D. Sluyter after J. Kamphuyzen. (ASKB)

◀ Napoleon shelters within a square of the Grenadiers of the Imperial Guard as the battle draws to its climax, while a staff officer appears to beseech him to flee. (Print after Charles Steuben)

▼ *Prussian Light Infantry: 1, NCO. Volunteer Jaeger Company, 9th Infantry Regiment (Colberg); 2, NCO, Volunteer Jaeger Company, 6th Infantry Regiment (1st West Prussian); 3, Volunteer Jaeger, 8th Infantry Regiment (Life Regiment). Volunteers were drawn largely from the middle classes and as such were able to provide themselves with attractive, good quality uniforms. (Bryan Fosten)*

◀ Napoleon's flight from the battlefield; his coach waits at the foot of the observation-tower.

▶ The meeting of Wellington and Blücher upon the field of victory on the evening of Waterloo, traditionally at La Belle Alliance; the old Prussian remarked 'Quelle affaire!' which, said Wellington, was about all the French he knew! (Painting by Adolph Menzel)

◀ 'La Garde meurt et ne se rend pas' – Cambronne's reputed reply to a call to surrender: the last stand of the Old Guard, attempting to delay the Allied pursuit in the last stage of the battle. (Print after Hippolyte Bellangé)

▶ Waterloo: the Morning after the Battle. J. H. Clark's graphic depiction of the wounded and dying lying unattended amid the slain reveals the full horror of the aftermath of a Napoleonic battle. Wives and children search the heaps of dead for their loved ones, scavengers rob the dead and dying, and a few small detachments attend to casualties. (ASKB)

that morning of the invincibility of British fire-power against a frontal attack had been proved all too accurate, even against the Imperial Guard. The battle was over, and with it Napoleon's chances of success. He fled back to Paris, where, drained once more into the lethargy that had haunted him at Ligny, after the exertions and reverses of the campaign, he renewed his abdication and retired to Malmaison.

The rest of the campaign would consist of a drive by the Allies into France itself, culminating at the gates of Paris. At the end of the day, the laurels of victory had gone to those who had made the fewer mistakes and on whom fortune and good staff work had smiled at the critical moments. Wellington had been able to survive his main strategic mistake at the start of the campaign by both the good fortune of Blücher's forward deployment and Ney's slowness both before and after the battle of Quatre Bras. He was not to give the French the opportunity to exploit a tactical error thereafter, and showed his customary but

unorthodox wisdom of concealing his forces from both the sight and the fire of the enemy. British and KGL coolness and firepower did the rest, aided by the general inability of the French properly to co-ordinate their assaults at Waterloo.

Blücher in turn had survived his main mistake of a dangerous forward concentration at Ligny by the French inability to bring either d'Erlon's or Lobau's Corps into the battle. Later the ability of the Prussians to reinforce Wellington at Waterloo was only even remotely possible by the fortuitous and almost accidental choice of Wavre as a rallying point for the Prussian army. Blücher's loyalty to Wellington and hatred of Napoleon did the rest, aided by Grouchy's late pursuit and determined observance of his equivocal orders.

All had seemed in Napoleon's favour at the start of the campaign, but success and eventual victory would depend upon how quickly his advantages were spent by his subordinates and on what returns he would get as they spent them. From the outset he was beset by problems that stemmed ultimately from his choices for command of the wings and his inexperienced general staff. Ney repeatedly squandered most of the advantage on the left wing for no return, and Napoleon let him do it. It must be said that the flash storm of the 17th did not help Napoleon either; but this would have had minimal effect on the Napoleon of Austerlitz or the Italian campaigns.

Even so, Napoleon almost succeeded. With a little more vigour on his part and a little closer supervision of Ney, the Prussians could have been pursued properly after Ligny and Wellington could have been defeated at Quatre Bras on the 17th instead of being permitted to extricate his army. The battle on the 18th, if it had happened at all, could have been over before the Prussians arrived.

◀ The village of Waterloo on the morning after the battle; at the right is the church, and at the left is the house in which Wellington wrote his dispatch; his ADC, Henry Percy, is departing to carry it home in the post-chaise. Allied wounded are being brought in. Engraving by T. Sutherland after a drawing made on the spot by 'A.M.S.'. (ASKB)

▶ The German Legion: 1, Hussar, 1st Hussar Regiment. This unit was 'converted' into lancers for the 1815 campaign but retained their hussar uniforms. 2, Gunner, Horse Artillery. (Bryan Fosten)

FINALE

There were still 120,000 Frenchmen in the field around Paris, and a further 150,000 conscripts in the depots. Already drained by the battles of the 18th, the Allied and Prussian armies became decidedly weaker as they advanced on Paris, leaving troops behind them to secure their lines of communication. For the French there was a very real opportunity to administer a quick reverse to the Allies around Paris: Davout urged Napoleon to try, but he was not to take it. The fighting was finally over.

Napoleon's political position in Paris was insecure in the face of a General Assembly led by Joseph Fouché, whom he had appointed Minister of Police but who was already in secret contact with the Allies and actively 'running both with the hare and with the hounds'. On 8 July, distrustful of Fouché, Napoleon set off to seek sanctuary in America. It was in the very nick of time, for Fouché had indeed ordered his arrest. The Royal Navy had been tipped off to intercept him, which they did, and on 15 July, expecting the very worst from the Chamber if he returned to Paris, Napoleon finally threw himself on the mercy of the Prince Regent and boarded HMS *Bellerophon*.

He was exiled to St. Helena, a remote, barren, rocky island in the South Atlantic with a poor climate. With his small entourage he lived in luxurious isolation, the mind that had tested the major powers of Europe now reduced to squabbling with the resident governor, which made his life an utter misery. There six years later he was to meet a premature death, perhaps, of all things, because of his choice of wallpaper (or so some would have us believe).

Others were not so lucky. Fouché issued a list that proscribed several of the generals who had supported Napoleon. Some, such as Lobau and Davout, were saved by the intervention of Wellington, but others were not. La Bedoyère, for example, met his fate in this way, and Marshal Ney, who had so fervently sought death during the closing stages of Waterloo, finally found it in the form of a firing squad after – typically – he had insisted on returning to Paris after Louis' restoration; had he waited just a few days longer before joining Napoleon, he would have cheated the firing squad, for upon reaching Belgium Louis dissolved his army, thereby releasing all officers from their oaths of allegiance.

Blücher rode in triumph through Paris, having at last avenged the indignities and atrocities inflicted on Prussia by Napoleon's 1806 campaign. He was narrowly thwarted in his avowed and determined intention to blow up the Pont de Jena in Paris, before returning to Prussia to spend the last four years of his life in a frenzy of hard drinking and wild gambling.

Wellington, meanwhile, had given the British army a stature unique since Marlborough and returned home a hero. He was heaped with honours from all around the world and festooned with riches – including the gift from the nation of Stratfield Saye House, near Reading, and £61,000 in prize money (privates received £2 11s 4d). He commanded the forces of occupation in France, following which he became Prime Minister from 1828 to 1830. He died in 1852.

THE BATTLEFIELD TODAY

Everyone should go to Waterloo at least once in his life. It is a unique amalgam of competing interests. At one level it is simply a huge tourist trap – the first theme park in Europe; at another it is a telling memorial to courage and wasted European life. Happily, either or both will guarantee the preservation of this magical site.

Visiting the site will take at least a day if you want to see it properly; half a day if you just want to tour the Allied positions for a swift overview. I believe that the best way to approach Waterloo is from the south along the N5 from either the E41 motorway or Charleroi itself. If you are coming from the E41, take the opportunity for a quick look at Fleurus and Ligny just north of the motorway on the next road along (the N21) before doubling back to the E41/N5. You will be amazed at just how small the Ligny stream is and the openness of the villages and the gently sloping terrain beyond.

Coming up the N5 you will pass through Frasnes-les-Gosselies, where Ney spent the night before Quatre Bras, and then you are almost upon the field of Quatre Bras itself. The old farmhouse of Gemioncourt is on the right next to the road and within sight of the N5/N49 crossroads. Stop at the side of the road for a few minutes and you will be standing at the very heart of the battle. Looking at the farmhouse itself, you can see why it took so long for the French to capture it. It is naturally strong, with high, windowless walls on all sides. Turning clockwise, just behind you will be the small ridge that you have just crossed, from where the French cannon bombarded the Allied positions, and from where the French main assaults were launched. Just to the west of the road is the plain where Kellerman began his desperate charge, across the insignificant ditch which divides the field. The field today stretches uninterrupted towards the west for a good distance, but in 1815

the Bois de Bossu – now just a clump of trees up by the main road – would have extended before you, channelling the French attacks up the slopes ahead. Just north of this central ditch on the far side is where the Brunswickers made their stand and where the young Duke met his fate. A gentle slope, which today offers a clear view of the forward slopes, at the time it was covered in man-height corn. One can understand Reille's caution as one turns to scan the Allied positions crossing the Brussels road just to the north. One can almost imagine the 92nd straddling the Brussels road itself, lancers swirling about the squares. The crossroads behind was the high-water mark of Ney's assaults, and to the east of the crossroads is the Namur Road from which Picton's Highlanders debouched to engage the French infantry columns behind Gemioncourt. It is all very compact, very visible and manageable for a general. The reality of short musketry range, the brutal effect of close-quarter volleys and cold steel and the total lack of control possible on anything beyond shouting distance – all particularly impress one at this site.

Back in the car, continue northwards along the N5, which bypasses Genappe, scene of the final rearguard action by Uxbridge and the horse batteries, and takes you past Le Caillou, Napoleon's HQ before the start of Waterloo and now a museum. Just a little way ahead and you arrive at La Belle Alliance, which is surrounded by memorials and monuments. Halt briefly at the side of the road to take your first glimpse of the panorama that faces you across the valley.

The most obvious feature opposite is the lump of earth that towers over the surrounding fields like a tumulus with a lion on the top. This is the Lion Mound, which marks the centre of the Allied position, and was erected after the battle and at the expense of the earth comprising the surrounding Allied ridge. To east and west of it stretches the ridge that marks Wellington's position, Papelotte to the east, the rooftops of Hougoumont perhaps just barely visible in its dip to the west. Tens of thousands of men literally packed into this tiny area. In front of the Lion Mound from where you are standing, glistening white on the main road itself, is La Haye Sainte, almost unchanged in more than 175 years, the ribbon-like Brussels Road undulating towards you. Monuments and memorials galore dot the field in a variety of styles, breaking the sky line.

Climb back into the car and head along the road to Wellington's positions. Once past La Haye Sainte, you can turn off the road to the right into a picnic area and car park; by turning left you come into a cluster of buildings that have gone up to service the tourist industry – cafés, souvenir shops, panorama paintings, several of the inevitable *fritures*, and a new and rather splendid visitors' centre. Somehow after wandering around this area one comes away with the distinct impression that our history books have made a mistake and that Napoleon actually won the battle!

To tour the field itself you will need a good pair of boots, for even in summer the ground gets soft and boggy, with a thick, grey mud that must have given real problems in 1815 after the night of drizzle and rain. Starting at the crossroads, you can see the height of the cutting the road makes on the eastern side, and which used to be similar on the other side before the raising of the Lion Mound caused it to be levelled off. Walk across to the picnic area to the east of the Brussels road and you will be standing in the deployment area of Kempt's brigade, in Picton's division. You can see the protection that must have been afforded by the ridge in the face of French cannon fire. Follow the footpath from the picnic area, which takes you towards the ridge and over the top, much as part of Kempt's brigade must have done, to see the commanding and inspiring view of the field that stretches to the French positions opposite. Just below you is where Donzelot struggled to deploy his lines, and where Kempt's brigades threw him back down the hill. Keeping to the side of the field, so as not to cause damage to crops, follow the slope down to where it runs alongside the Brussels road opposite La Haye Sainte, which has a memorial

plaque. They certainly build their farmhouses strong in Belgium. Can they be musket ball marks in the wall? The original orchard to the south is no longer there.

On your side of the road you are standing on what was a gravel pit, occupied at the start of the day by the 95th Rifles, now filled in. Moving on just a little way, just below the southernmost end of La Haye Sainte, you may still be lucky enough to find a track into the field at the bottom of the hill. Walking along this a little way you are at the very bottom of the valley, the site of frenzied cavalry charges by the British dragoons, and the Cuirassiers and Red Lancers who repelled them. The steepness of the slope is at once apparent, as is the realization that there is something of a dip on either side of the Brussels road, for whatever is happening on the far side of it cannot be seen from this side of the valley. Back to the road – lined with poplar trees in 1815 – head down to La Belle Alliance, passing on the left both the initial and final positions of the French batteries. At la Belle Alliance take the turning to the left to Plancenoit, and a few yards along it on the right are some steps to take you up to Napoleon's vantage point. From here you can see nearly all of the Allied lines. Interestingly, the part of the field that is not visible is Hougoumont and its environs. Is this the reason why Jérôme was given such a free hand, perhaps? To the right can be seen the woods of the Bois de Paris and the hills upon which they rest.

Carry on along the road to Plancenoit past some pretty, modern houses, and into the village itself. It will be immediately apparent just how open and spacious the village centre is. A visit to the Prussian memorial is worth the effort (it is signposted), and in the village itself there is a very friendly bar/cafe.

Returning to La Belle Alliance, there is a French memorial depicting a dying eagle, and for some reason a monument to Victor Hugo, who wrote about the battle in none-too-accurate terms. Almost opposite the road to Plancenoit is a track that takes you from La Belle Alliance over in the approximate direction of Hougoumont, and more or less parallel with the Allied positions. (This is where you may be glad you took the boots I mentioned earlier.) Within a very short distance the route dips into a hollow, and by the time you reach a point opposite the centre of the Allied line not even the roof of La Belle Alliance can be seen, nor anything on the eastern side of the Brussels road. Totally 'out of sight', you are now standing in the area where the French cavalry got out of hand and, instead of a few squadrons advancing, whole regiments almost spontaneously charged the centre of the Allied line ahead of you. Perhaps standing here we can appreciate how the sheer problem of visibility could have been a contribution to the loss of control.

You are also following the route taken by the Imperial Guard for their last assault on the Allied centre, and to follow this key part of the battle you should now leave the track and head for the centre of the Allied positions. As you reach the crest, the long and gentle slope of the reverse side of the ridge shows what a superb defensive position this was for Wellington's infantry to mass – plenty of space, good lines of sight and the opportunity to interlock lines of fire. Breasting the crest to see the slope behind massed with infantry must have been a demoralizing sight indeed. Today a section of motorway crosses a part of the site – roughly where Somerset's brigade stood at the start of the battle.

At the Ohain road which traverses the crest, it is clear that the roadway at this part of the line was not 'sunken' to the extent of presenting an obstacle to troops crossing it. At the crest is a sign indicating the position of Mercer's cannon during the latter part of the battle. You are now almost in the cluster of buildings at the centre of the Allied lines once more.

Here, the panorama is worth a visit. This is a large circular building with an old, rather dusty but still very impressive painting all the way around the inside. The idea is that you are on that very spot in the middle of the Allied line at 4 p.m. or so on the day of the battle. As you stand amid the Allied artillery and looking back up the slope, ahead of you and to the side are British battalions; to your left and right are the near life-size Dragoons of the Guard and Lancers of the Guard dramatically breasting the crest of the ridge, spurring onwards; and all around you are the Cuirassiers of l'Héritier's division, attacking a battery of guns. Large models and military impedimenta serve to blend the edge between you and the painting, and a true sense of excitement is expressed in the painting style.

The newly constructed visitors' centre nearby shows scenes from *Waterloo*, the motion picture of the battle, together with a model of the battlefield area. In the low lighting levels of the cinema atmosphere, movements during the various stages of the battle are shown on the model by means of coloured lights. Attached to the visitors' centre is the Lion Mound itself. The steps going up to the top seem to go on for ever, but the view from the top is a very pleasant one. To see the battlefield properly, though, you have to walk all over it. It all looks flat from up here!

The final port of call is Hougoumont itself, which, if you do not have much time left can be visited by car on the way out. It is signposted from the south-bound carriageway of the N6 by crossed sabres over the 1815 date. It is another strongly built building, but this time on an even grander scale.

I doubt whether one would have time to visit Wavre unless on a two-day tour of the area. If you want to try it, however, the way to go is from the battlefield of Waterloo itself to Lasne, either along the Ohain road (which takes you past Papelotte and La Haie) or from Plancenoit – the roads join halfway there. Lasne and its neighbouring village, Chapelle St. Lambert, are in the Bois de Paris, and a variety of small roads will take you to Limale, Bierges and on to Wavre – all scenes of hard fighting. The terrain is very hilly; even today it is not a very easy journey, and it is easy to get lost. In 1815 with the added problem of heavy mud it must have been much more difficult. There is plenty of parking at Wavre town centre, and the town itself is worth a visit for an hour or two. The Dyle at Wavre is a formidable obstacle, and it is no wonder Grouchy bypassed it by striking at Limale.

CHRONOLOGY

1814 Napoleon's exile to Elba; Congress of Vienna

1815:
1 March Napoleon returns to France
13 March Allies declare him an outlaw
20 March Napoleon enters Paris
25 March Allies declare war on him; mobilization and recruitment begin; rebellion in the Vendée

15 June: 3.00 Armée du Nord commences crossing of the Sambre
3.30 Ney arrives at Charleroi to join the campaign; Napoleon gives him command of a wing
17.30 Napoleon engages Prussian rearguard at Gilly; Wellington receives news from Gneisenau of a 'major attack by the French'
18.30 Ney takes Frasnes
20.00 Napoleon returns to Charleroi, exhausted; Wellington and his staff attend Duchess of Richmond's ball

16 June: 4.00 The Emperor rises
6.00 Prussians seen to be moving on Brye/St. Amand
9.30 Wellington arrives at Quatre Bras to see the French preparing a meal and Ney still awaiting orders at Quatre Bras; Blücher is now at Brye
11.00 The Emperor arrives at Fleurus with the Guard
12.00 Wellington meets Blücher at Brye
14.00 Battles of Ligny and Quatre Bras commence

The Battle of Quatre Bras: 15.00 French main advance checked by arrival of Picton
16.00 Ney's all-out assault; d'Erlon ordered to Ligny
17.00 Kellermann's charge
17.30 Alten's attack
19.00 British Guards retake Bossu Wood; Wellington's counter-attack

21.00 Battle ends with opposing forces at their original positions; d'Erlon returns to Fleurus

The Battle of Ligny: 15.00 First Assaults on Prussian-held villages
17.00 Wagnele, St. Amand and La Haye Sainte fall to the French
17.30 Tongrinelle falls to the French; Ligny still bitterly contested.
18.00 Napoleon orders up the Guard; d'Erlon arrives behind the French flank; Blücher retakes St. Amand
19.00 D'Erlon marches off to rejoin Ney; the Guard begins attack on Ligny; St. Amand retaken
20.30 The Guard breaks through the Prussian centre; Blücher injured
21.00 The Emperor returns to Fleurus, exhausted, possibly ill; he refuses to receive Grouchy later that night.
17 June: 2.00 Sombreffe finally evacuated by last of the Prussians
5.00 Wellington dispatches ADC Gordon to determine outcome of Ligny
8.00 The Emperor comes down to breakfast; orders troops to prepare for inspection
9.30 Blücher confirms Wavre as destination of retreat to Gneisenau and Gordon; Napoleon tours the battlefield of Ligny
10.30 Wellington begins withdrawal from Quatre Bras
11.00 Napoleon receives a report from Ney and orders him to attack Wellington; Grouchy is to pursue Blücher
12.00 Last of Wellington's infantry leave Quatre Bras
13.00 Grouchy starts pursuit of the Prussians
14.30 Napoleon arrives at Quatre Bras to find only British cavalry rearguard remaining and Ney's troops eating lunch; a thunderstorm breaks
15.00 Grouchy arrives at Point du Jour, one mile

east of Ligny; he orders Vandamme to Gembloux

18.30 Napoleon's advance guard reaches La Belle Alliance

20.00 The head of Vandamme's corps arrives at Gembloux, six miles from Point du Jour; there is no sign of the Prussians; the army bivouacs

18 June: The Battle of Waterloo:

3.30 Wellington receives confirmation from Blücher that he will come to his aid; Wellington confirms his stand at Mont St. Jean

3.48 Dawn; the Prussian IV Corps breaks camp near Wavre.

9.00 Wellington's deployment complete

10.00 Napoleon orders his final dispositions

11.30 24-gun bombardment of Allied lines; assault on Hougoumont begins

11.45 Grouchy decides not to march to the sound of the guns

12.00 Prussian hussar captured near St. Lambert, three miles from La Belle Alliance; Lobau deployed to guard the French right flank

13.00 French bombardment increased; now 88 guns, two to three rounds per minute

13.30 D'Erlon's assault on Picton, with Travers and Dubois in support; assault held; Kempt countercharges; death of Picton

14.00 Travers and Dubois descend on Kempt and Pack; Uxbridge counter-charges with two British heavy cavalry brigades; elements charge the French cannon and are repulsed with heavy loss

16.00 Prussian IV Corps advance guard emerges from the Bois de Paris; Lobau checks the Prussian advance; start of mass attacks by French cavalry on Allied right centre

17.00 Remainder of French cavalry committed; Prussian II corps arrives on left of IV Corps

17.30 Arrival of Reille's infantry in support of now-spent French cavalry attack on Allied centre broken up with heavy losses on both sides; Lobau defends Plancenoit in a desperate struggle

18.00 Ney organizes a third assault on Wellington's centre; the Young Guard is sent in to Plancenoit; Old Guard deployed behind Lobau in support

18.30 Prussians thrown out of Plancenoit; Prussians pause to regroup; La Haye Sainte falls to Ney; British centre is open; Wellington in crisis; Ney asks for reinforcements

18.45 Arrival of Prussian I Corps near Wellington's left allows him to contract his line

19.00 Imperial Guard brought back into Reserve; Chassé arrives to plug the gap in Wellington's line; Wellington brings up his last reserves (Brunswickers) personally

19.30 Assault of the Guard on Wellington's right centre

20.15 All Guard attacks have been repelled; Prussian I Corps now engaged

21.00 Plancenoit retaken by the Prussians; last stand of the Guard

21.30 Prussians at Rossomme

22.00 Wellington and Blucher meet at La Belle Alliance

Wavre 18-19 June:

Grouchy attacks and eventually defeats Prussian III Corps around Wavre; upon hearing the outcome of the Battle of Waterloo, Grouchy withdraws to France

21 June Napoleon arrives back in Paris

15 July Napoleon surrenders aboard HMS *Bellerophon*

A GUIDE TO
FURTHER READING

Barrès, J.-B. *Memoirs of a French Napoleonic Officer.* London, 1925, 1988.

Bowden, S. *Armies at Waterloo,* Arlington, 1983.

Chandler, D. G. *The Campaigns of Napoleon.* New York 1966, London 1967.

Waterloo: *The Hundred Days.* London, 1980.

Coignet, J.-R. *The Note Books of Captain Coignet.* London, 1985; first published as *Captain Coignet: Soldier of the Empire.* London, 1897, 1928.

Esposito, V. J. and J. R. Elting. *A Military History and Atlas of the Napoleonic Wars.* New York, 1964: London and New York, 1980.

Fuller, J. F. C. *The Decisive Battles of the Western World.* 2 volumes, London, 1954–6.

Glover, M. *Wellington as Military Commander.* London, 1973.

— *Battlefields of Northern France.* London, 1987.

Haythornthwaite, P. J. *Uniforms of Waterloo.* London, 1974.

— *Napoleon's Military Machine.* London, 1988.

Lachouque, H. *Waterloo.* Paris, 1972; London and New York, 1975.

Mann, M. *And they Rode On.* Salisbury, 1984.

Maxwell, H. *The Life of Wellington.* London, 1899.

Mercer, C. *Journal of the Waterloo Campaign.* London, 1870.

Naylor, J. *Waterloo.* London, 1960.

Pivka, O. von. *Armies of the Napoleonic Wars.* Newton Abbot, 1979.

Siborne, W. *History of the Waterloo Campaign.* London, 1848, 1990.

Sutherland, J. *Men of Waterloo.* London, 1966.

Weller, J. *Wellington at Waterloo.* London, 1967, 1992.

INDEX

(References to illustrations are shown in **bold**.)